FOREX

SWING TRADING

THE SECRET STRATEGIES FOR CREATING
A PASSIVE INCOME FOR A LIVING IN A SIMPLE GUIDE.

DAY AND SWING TECHNIQUES,
PSYCHOLOGY, TIPS & TRICKS, DISCIPLINE,

FOR BEGINNERS

Table of Contents

Introduction

There is a lot of confusion out there about what swing trading really is. So, let me be very clear on what it is.

Swing trading is a short-term trading style that involves you taking a position in the financial markets and staying with it for a number of days, perhaps weeks. So, you could watch American Express stock today and decide that you are going to buy it, then after you place your trade, you let it stay for a day or two, perhaps even more depending on how fast the market action is and the time frame you are watching.

Swing trading is different from other types of trading such as position trading, day trading, high frequency trading or scalping mainly because of the period of time that a trade is held. On one hand, some trading styles such as position trading allow you to take a position and then hold it for a longer period of time such as a couple of months or even years. On the other hand, a style such as scalping can involve holding a position for a few minutes, perhaps even seconds. Therefore, a good way to think about swing trading is, a style that strikes a balance between both sides, offering more flexibility.

As a swing trader, you are mainly looking to profit from short term price changes or what is known as price swings in the markets. Now that we have fully defined what swing trading is, let us compare it to "Day trading."

Swing trading vs. Day trading

As I said before, many people who are new to trading ask themselves, "What is the difference between Swing trading and Day trading?" So, let's talk about it. Day trading is a completely different trading style. And the difference between the two comes down to the length of time that positions are held. Day trading is a trading style in which you execute a number of positions in a day, but at the end of the day, you close all of them out. So, you may open a number of trades, say 10 of them in a day, but at the end of the day, you are flat.

You will never find a day trader holding a position overnight, the way you may find swing traders or position traders doing. A day trader prefers to take small daily gains from the market consistently but not hold his positions for any longer than a day. Because of this, you will often find day traders seeking opportunities in short time frames such as one minute, five minutes, ten minutes or even 30 minutes.

If you think about it, day trading is more like a day job. As a matter of fact, most hot shot day traders simply regard it as their main source of income.

Swing trading is regarded as more of a part time activity. In swing trading, you will be typically looking at longer time frames such as 3 hours, 4 hours, daily or weekly to spot swing trading opportunities. Therefore, this type of trading can be adopted by people who are already employed in a different job.

If for instance you are a swing trader who is looking at a 4-hour chart to trade, this means that a single candlestick in a candlestick chart will be formed every four hours. This means that you only need to check up your chart every four hours to see what is going on. So, if you are an employee, even with a busy schedule, my guess is you can still afford to check up a chart every four hours. So, this type of trading style can suit you.

Another thing to keep in mind is that, since day trading involves placing trades every now and then, the natural ups and downs of the markets can end up being very stressful indeed. A small mistake in this type of trading can end up wiping you out on all your profits. So, day trading can only suit you if you are someone who is very disciplined and can withstand short term ups and downs in your portfolio.

Swing trading allows you take a more laidback approach. You can place a trade and walk away from your computer and not have to worry about it until may be the next day. So, if your goal is to seek a source of income that is more passive, then swing trading is the way to go. It is also good for you if you are a person of mild temperament who doesn't like lots of action.

Truth be told, none of these trading styles is better than the other. It is just a matter of picking the trading style that fits you as a person and your current situation in life. You may want to consider the following before you make a decision:

The amount of time that you can set aside for trading: If you are a busy person, you may want to consider swing trading.

The amount of money that you have: Day trading may require that you start out with a lot of money since you will end up being dependent on it for your means of livelihood.

Your personality: If you are more of a person who likes to take things nice and slow, you may want to stay away from day trading and opt for swing trading instead.

Risk tolerance: Day trading is for you if you can withstand watching several trades going against you and still maintain your calmness. Swing trading is better if you are more of the calculating type who can only stand taking a loss once in a while.

Trading experience: Trading experience matters a lot in trading. If you are new to trading, you may need to start as a swing trader and take your time to learn the ropes. After you start mastering the business, you can then slowly graduate to day trading. Day trading is meant for competent professionals who have a lot of experience in this business and therefore know what they are doing.

Now that you have fully understood what Swing trading is and how different it is from Day trading; it is time that we began looking into a number of Swing trading strategies that you can apply.

Chapter 1. General Introduction to Forex

Forex market is a market where you will buy, sell, exchange as well as speculate on the currencies. The market comprises of banks, retail forex brokers, hedge funds, central banks as well as investors. The currency market tends to be a financial market that has a tremendous amount of transactions, exceeding the combination of equity markets and futures. It is the most liquid of all the markets and the currencies are traded against one another. Exchanging currencies is one of the most crucial things since that has to be there if people need to do foreign trade as well as business.

Despite being among the most significant markets, there is no physical centralized site where the exchanges takes place. All transactions are done over-the-counter. The market is always open, and it is so all over the world. You will find that the market is still active during day time and the price quotes change from time to time. The transactions will happen so that one can have a financial advantage. The fact that individual currency varies is what will make the need for foreign exchange to raise.

When it comes to conducting trade, commercial as well as investment banks are in charge of doing that on their client's behalf. There are cases when individual and professional investors have the opportunity to trade in currency. But it is challenging for them, and it gives them a tough time. The internet has helped individual traders know more about the forex market.

Someone who is getting into the market for the first time, will find it risky as well as complex to handle. There are different regulations, and a standardization of the forex instruments. In some parts of the world you can come across markets that have no rules. The banks in the trade will determine and accept only the risks they are willing to take, since they need to make sure that they will not suffer huge losses. The banks will impose regulations that will work best for them.

Any bank that is willing to be a part of the forex market will provide offers for currency and currency pairs. How the bank determines prices will depend on the demand for a currency or currency pair in the market and the amount they can afford to supply. Traders can in no way influence prices because of the system's large trade flow. This is vital for creating transparency.

Small retail traders can be tempted to use unregulated brokers who will re-quote the bank prices if and when they wish to do so. In some cases, they might even trade against their customers and take advantage. Depending on where you and your broker are based there might or might not be regulations. The rules are not consistent all over the world. In order to know whether your broker is under regulation or not, you need to perform a thorough research. When deciding on which broker firm to go with, look at the ask and the bid price that the broker quotes, and other important aspects including the margin and the leverage level that they offer. Watch out for complaints from customers about not being able to withdraw funds Always work only with regulated brokers and seek the kind of protection that will work in your favor in case a crisis arises or the broker becomes insolvent.

While the concept of forex trading is easy, executing your trades on the market is difficult. This doesn't mean you won't become successful. What it means is that you will need to educate yourself and work hard. The first step anyone should take is to learn as much as possible about forex trading.

Concepts of forex trading

The majors

The very first concept that you must understand is the majors. The majors refer to the major currencies that are regularly traded in the Forex market. The stock market has thousands of shares that the trader can choose from to invest in. This more often than not ends up confusing the trader and might also cause them to make the wrong investments. But this problem is tackled in the Forex market, as there are certain major currencies that you can trade in on a regular basis. These are based on trends and after understanding which countries provide you with the best overvalued and undervalued advantages. Here is the list of the 8 major countries that you can turn to in order remain with the highest profit.

The United States of America
Canada
Europe
United Kingdom
Switzerland
Australia
New Zealand
Japan

These countries and their currencies are identified as the big 8 because they have the best financial markets and/or manufacturing capabilities. These facts allow their currencies to always remain in demand for exchange. If you exchange any of these currencies in the right moment, your investment will surely be safe. For that, you have to constantly follow the economic scene of all the individual countries.

Buy and sell

You have to understand that the Forex market works in a simultaneous buying and selling fashion. This means that if you want to buy one currency, you will have to sell the one you have at the same time. This is easy to understand if you have, for example, physical Euros, and walk into a Bank and exchange for physical Dollars. You sell your Euros and purchased Dollars. One transaction that includes buy and sell.

But in the Forex world, we trade Forex symbols called "pairs." So, when you are buying one currency, you will automatically be selling another. In the simple example mentioned above, you traded the pair EUR/USD. In a trading platform, you use this symbol if you want to buy Euros (in Dollars) or Dollars (in Euros). All pairs or symbols have the same principle. If you "buy the symbol" you are buying the first currency if you "sell the symbol" you are buying the second currency. You have to get used to this concept in order to trade in Forex. You will have to calculate the basis points of the currencies based on their difference. That you can calculate by looking at the trending rates of the two currencies. The basis points refer to a measure of the interest or any percentages that you need to calculate before you go ahead with a deal. You will be able to calculate your gain by doing so.

Rate of return

The rate of return in the forex market is quite large. This means that you can remain with a big profit or a big loss depending on your investment. There have been cases of people making millions by just investing a few hundred or thousand dollars. This is possible if you know to invest in the market the right way. Let's say you invest $10 in the market and it gives you a return of $1000. That is highly possible in the currency market. However, if you get it wrong, then you might end up losing a lot of money. The currency market is extremely volatile, and you have to remain abreast of the difference in values of the currencies. The idea is to look for currencies that are momentarily undervalued, that way, you can expect a big change in value to finally close the transaction at your desired profit. If at any time you feel that the prices of the currencies are going to cause you a loss, then you must sell them off.

Dual benefits

The forex market offers you dual benefits when you invest in the market. It is better known as the Currency Carry Trade. The Currency Carry Trade is one where the person stands to benefit in two ways. Let us look at an example. Now let's say a Chinese trader exchanges 5000 Yuan for dollars and buys a bond with the dollars' worth. The trader will receive an interest of 5% on the bond provided the rate of exchange between the two countries remains the same. If it does, then the trader will stand to gain a profit of 50% owing to the difference in the currency values. This is an added benefit to the fact that the trader will also be able to avail a profit from selling the bond later. Here, you have to understand that the exchange rate between the two should remain the same otherwise the trader will lose money. This risk is quite high with currencies whose rates are quite volatile. You will not be able to predict the difference in rates, and by the time you withdraw from it, you probably would have lost quite some money. The difference in the rates usually occurs over a period of years and will not be within a short period of time.

OTC

Unlike the regular Stock Market (that deals with regulated Financial Instruments), Forex is always traded OTC (over the counter). This means that the currencies are not considered "financial instruments" in most countries and are not regulated as such. Banks and Brokers trade currencies via an Electronic Communication Network (ECN). A medium that is different from a stock market exchange like NYSE or AMEX. A dealer will be responsible for the trade, and there will be no centralized control over the trade. It is the same manner in which penny stocks and bonds are exchanged. You will have to do some homework on how you can start trading in your local market as the method differs from country to country. You have to look at dealers that will help you get these currencies. All Banks and Brokers, authorized to exchange, are connected to this network. In essence, you need an authorized bank or broker to handle your orders via the internet. These form the different basic concepts of forex that you have to understand if you wish to trade in it. They will act as your guide when you partake in forex trading.

Understanding Pairs

The main difference between the stock market and the forex market is that, in forex, you are essentially trading pairs of currency (that is you buy one currency and sell another), while in the stock market, you buy shares of a company. This is not an option when you are forex trading. Whether you are trading, selling, or buying, you have to use pairs. For example, the Japanese yen is often paired against the Canadian dollar and the Euro against the American dollar.

What's a Pip?

A pip is a 1% movement in the currency value. A pip is a basic unit that is used when talking about currency quotes. It is the last number of the quote, so when you are following the movement of two currencies, you look at the last two digits so that you can say that a currency moved by the number of pips that differentiates the second from the starting figure. The value of the pip is determined from the size of the trade. You make a decision to buy or sell a currency pair depending on your evaluation, which is when you make the market order.

Currency prices typically move in such tiny increments that they are quoted in pips or percentage in point. In most cases, a pip refers to the fourth decimal point of a price that is equal to 1/100th of 1%.

If the EUR/USD moves from 1.0946 to 1.0947 the .0001 USD rise in value is equal to one pip.

Fractional Pips

The superscript number at the end of each price is the Fractional Pip, which is 1/10th of a pip. The fractional pip provides even more precise indication of price movements.

If the EUR/USD moves from 1.0947 to 1.0957

it **increased by 10 pips**

If the EUR/USD moves from 1.0947 to 1.0937

it **decreases by 10 pips**

Things are different for the Japanese yen (JPY) which is quoted to two decimal points:

If the USD/JPY moves from 107.64 to 107.84

it **increases by 20 pips**

If the USD/JPY moves from 107.64 to 107.44

it **decreases by 20 pips**

The value of a pip varies based on the currency pairs that you are trading and depends on which currency is the base currency and which is the counter currency.

For example

EUR/USD

If the U.S. dollar is on the right side of the pair (the counter side) then one pip is valued at $1USD per 10,000 traded

(pip size) x (base currency) = pip value

(1 pip) x (10,000 euros) = $1USD

Therefore:

if you buy 10,000 euros against the US dollar (EUR/USD) at 1.10440 and you earn 1 dollar for every pip increase in your favor, if you sold at 1.10540 (10 pip increase) you would earn 10$.

If the circumstances were the same but you sold at 1.10340 (10 pip decrease) you would lose 10$.

Let's look at an example with USD as base currency and JPY as counter currency.

In this case the value of one pip depends on the USD/JPY exchange rate.

Let's imagine the buy price for USD/JPY is 107.64 and lot size is 10.000

(pip size)/(exchange rate)x(base currency) = pip value

(1 pip/(107.64) x (10,000 USD) = .93 USD

If you buy 10,000 USD against the Japanese yen at 107.64 and you make 0.93$ for every pip increase, if you sold at 107.84 (a 20 pip increase) you would make 18.6$

On the other hand, if you sold at 107.44 (a 20 pip decrease) you would lose 18.6$

Entry Order

When you use an entry order, you enter your currency pair trade at a specific price. If the price of the currency never reaches the specific price, then your trade is not enforced. If the price is reached, then your trade is completed regardless of your presence at the time.

Stop-Loss Order

A stop-loss order is the price at which you want your dealer to exit the trade when the trade moves against your interests. A stop-loss order prevents losses.

Take profit order

A take profit order is an order that closes your trade once it reaches a certain level of profit. When your take profit order is hit on a trade, the trade is closed at the current market value. Take profit orders are also sometimes referred to as limit orders.

Limit

A limit is the price at which you want the dealer to exit the trade when it's moving in your favor. Knowing when to exit the trade even when things are looking up is useful because you can hardly predict when a currency will start to drop.

Technically a limit order is an order to buy or sell at a specified price or better. A sell limit order is filled at the specified price or higher; buy limit orders are executed at the specified price or lower.

The limit order allows traders to better control the prices they trade. By using a buy limit order, the investor is guaranteed to pay that price or less. While the price is guaranteed, the filling of the order is not, and limit orders will not be executed unless the price meets the order qualifications. If the asset does not reach the specified price, the order is not filled and the investor may miss out on the trading opportunity.

Margin

When you are buying or selling at a good margin, that means that you control a large amount of currency for an initial investment that is way smaller in comparison. For example, a 100-by-1 margin means that you invest $1,000 for a trade of $100,000. Buying and selling on a margin is safe and appealing because the only amount you risk to lose is the amount you invested, but you have the opportunity to profit a greater amount.

Leveraging Ratios

You are betting at leveraging ratios. A $1,000 bet on 1,000 value of the currency is considered 1:1 leverage.

Trading platforms allow you to follow and market currency in a way that creates a profit. When you're successful in trading one currency so that its value increases against the currency you used to buy it, you can make a profit. You are speculating whether the currency will rise or drop. Your chances of profiting essentially increase with the success of your predictions.

With forex, you trade using leverage, which means that you only need to invest a portion of your positions. By using stop-losses, you can prevent losing your investment.

When it comes to currency rates, many factors have an influence. Interest rates, unemployment numbers, political events, and many more affect the country's currency value.

Currencies may rise and fall in different values for different reasons, one of them being large companies exchanging currencies for the purpose of international trading. The time and circulation of market information is also a significant factor. False and accurate information circulating the market can influence banks to swiftly market currencies, which additionally affects the changes in currency values.

Diversification

You want to ensure you have diversity within your portfolio to tackle risk. In fact, because the forex market is open 24 hours a day during the weekdays, the market holds more diversity. Therefore, don't just focus on the popular currencies, such as the American dollar and Canadian dollar. You may also trade other pairs such as American dollar/British pound (USD/GBP) or American dollar/Japanese Yen (USD/JPY).

What Are the Risks?

While there are many people trading in forex, there are also those who are facing major financial losses. Since forex trading is essentially all about predictions, one of the biggest risks, obviously, is making a wrong prediction. The following are the many risks of forex trading.

The Wrong Mindset

When it comes to any market, you always need to have the right mindset. Take a moment to think about how certain emotions, such as fear or worry, can control your thoughts. You have to find a way to keep your emotions out of the market. Experienced traders call the right mindset the winning mindset. The following are some key characteristics that will help you gain your winning attitude.

You need to be self-disciplined. You want to make sure that you take all the steps to ensure you are doing what you need to do to reach success. This means that you complete daily research to see how the forex market is doing, and you document all your currencies, trades, and any other information. Fortunately, most marketing platforms keep your information in its history. However, it is always best that you find a way to keep the files on your computer so that you always have them. You follow any rules and guidelines that your mentor or yourself have set up.

You are also able to keep your emotions in check. This might mean that you follow certain strategies you set up for yourself, such as deep-breathing exercises. You don't allow yourself to give in to your excitement if a trade goes well or when you see your account balance. While you might smile and be proud of yourself, you don't allow the feeling to take over as you can become too confident. This can lead you to make mistakes, which can put you and your finances in jeopardy.

You understand that mistakes are going to be made. Instead of focusing on your mistakes and allowing them to control your future decisions, you learn from them. Many traders write down their mistakes in their trading journal or daily reports.

You understand that the market is fluid and are able to adjust to the changes. For instance, if a price notes that you need to make a change in your portfolio, then you make a change. Your portfolio is the place where you keep all the currencies that you can sell or trade.

You understand your risk tolerance. No matter what strategies you use to try to limit your risk, there is always a risk. If you aren't comfortable with a lot of risks, you will want to focus more on trades that are low risk.

Currency-Value Fluctuations

There are internal-market reasons and external reasons for a currency's value changes. Internally, one country's currency can increase while another currency you hold decreases. These fluctuations are often dependent on how many people are buying and selling the currency. For example, if the yen isn't strong, then more people will purchase the yen, which makes the value increase. This could show a decrease in the American dollar in comparison to the yen because traders are using the American dollar to purchase yen. In other words, the more people purchase currency, the stronger its value. The more people sell a currency, the lower its value.

External factors can be anything from politics to other events going on within the country. These are factors that traders cannot control but you should always be aware of. Because of this, many traders will spend at least half an hour every morning going through the news in order to get an idea of what the market is going to look like that day. Doing this will allow you to know if you should purchase a currency or trade one within your portfolio.

Broker Risk

While not every trader has a broker, it is important for a beginner to look into a broker. This person can help you learn about the market and give you advice on what moves to take. However, there are broker risks. In order to limit these risks, you want to ensure you can trust your broker. Do some research before you decide to take on a broker. The best way you can do this is by choosing a broker who is part of a government body as it is regulated. Government bodies have to follow guidelines and ethics.

How to Start

Whenever you start trading, you want to ensure you follow certain steps for success. First, you always want to do your research. You want to learn as much as possible. This means you will read books, join forex trading forums, find a trusted broker, and anything else you feel is necessary. Once you feel like you know forex trading like the back of your hand, you will be able to move on.

Second, ensure you understand the language. Forex trading has its own language. Take your time to learn these terms, and if you have questions, find another trader to discuss your concerns with.

Third, you want to find your trusted broker. This person will help you make decisions and explain the world of investing to you. Take your time to find the best broker for you. Your broker will help you set up an account.

Fourth, take time to analyze the forex market. Learn about the charts and what they mean. Look back in the history of some currencies so you can gain a better understanding of trading. For example, charts can help you analyze the best time for trading and which currencies are best within the market and help you find the best currencies.

Fifth, if you are trading full-time, set up an office and your schedule. You want to find time to ensure you are self-disciplined enough that you won't struggle with distractions. Take the time to set a start date.

Sixth, once your day arrives, start trading. Make sure that you go through your morning routine, such as reading the paper and seeing how the currencies are doing. Notice any changes that occurred overnight. You also want to ensure you go through your daily schedule and close out your day with your evening routine. For example, check your stocks for the day, and discuss anything about your day in your journal.

How to Profit

Once you start trading, you will want to do what you can to limit your risks. While you will always have some risk, you can find a comfortable level of risk. Another way to profit is by diversifying your portfolio. This means that you will have different currencies and not focus on the same ones.

You also want to be patient. Forex trading is not a get-rich-quick scheme. It will take time to start seeing a profit. Don't give up, and don't fall into the wrong mindset. If you need any help, talk to your broker, a mentor, or someone in the forum. There are many experienced forex traders who are happy to help beginners.

Continue to communicate with your broker, mentor, and anyone on the forum. Even if you spend months researching, people will always be important when it comes to your success. Don't allow yourself to get into the mindset that you know everything. Continue to learn as much as possible. Take time to practice analyzing reports. You have to do whatever you need to so you feel comfortable as a trader.

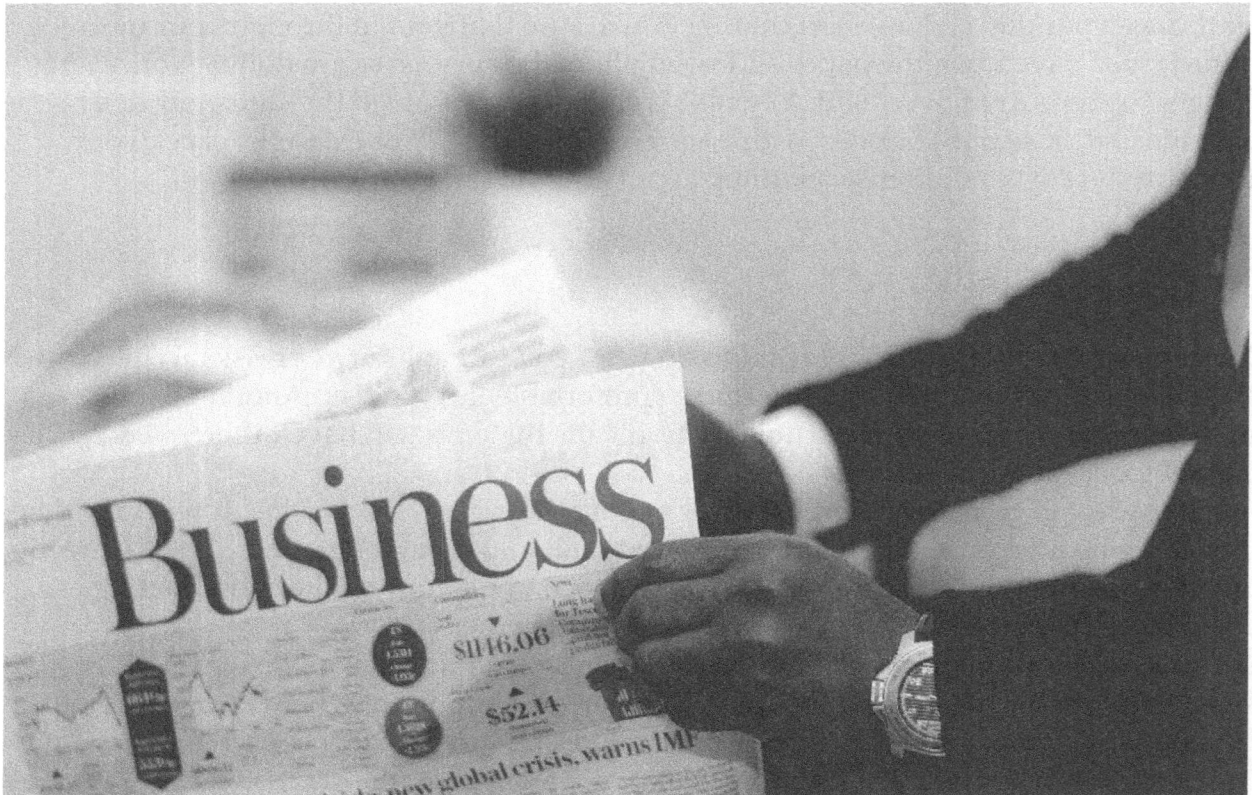

Forex Trading Pros and Cons

Forex trading has many favorable aspects, but just like every other trading activity, it has a downside. Every trader that seeks to enter the trade system must assess the advantages and disadvantages of foreign exchange before they make a decision in the appropriateness and attractiveness of the market.

Advantages

Forex exchange has a large number of advantages regardless of the risks; therefore, it makes an attractive and lucrative activity.

The advantages include:

Leverage

Leverage provides traders with substantial opportunities for them to trade and make profits. Access to leverage largely determines the difference between small profits and large ones. In the foreign exchange market, there are more resources for leverage than other markets and depending on the location from which a trader is working from one can get the resource they need. A trader may be able to access a margin that supports leverage of 100:1 or more for the initial capital.

Fast returns

The foreign exchange market moves very fast, and the liquidity is very deep. When the speed, liquidity, and high leverage are combined in the forex market, they create great opportunities for the trader to make exponential profits in the trade more than other markets. In some other markets, the traders have to wait for very long and still get limited returns.

Easy "short selling"

In some other markets, short selling may require a trader to borrow assets and get exposed to risks, but in the forex exchange, short selling currencies have a simpler process. Foreign exchange works in a way that the trader buys one currency while selling the other. In other words, the currencies are traded in pairs. Traders speculate the inclines and declines of different currencies, therefore, sell the losing currency and buy the winning pair without involving a borrowing process.

Liquidity

Because the forex market is the largest market in the world by volume, there are many participants; therefore, liquidity for trading is ample especially for the major currencies. Liquidity allows the traders to buy and sell the currencies quickly at any time; there is a flow of traders in the market. A large number of participants in the market enable the trader to transact extremely large orders of currencies without diverting the prices too much. Liquidity reduces the chances of price anomalies and manipulation, and as such, the spreads become tighter leading to efficient pricing. A trader does not have to worry about the stagnant prices during the afternoon and high volatility during the opening and closing which constantly affect the equity markets. In the forex market, a trader can observe similarities in the patterns of volatility (low, mid and high) apart from times when major events occur.

Lack of central exchange

Keeping in mind that the forex exchange market operates globally, there is no central regulatory or centralized exchange. The market operates as an over the counter although central banks occasionally interfere with the operations as needed in order to regulate it. However, it is very rare for the central banks of any other authority to intervene unless under extreme conditions. The decentralization and deregulation of the market ensure that the traders are safe from sudden surprises. Many of the other security markets are centralized for example the equity market. When a company trading in the equity market suddenly reports losses or declares a dividend, the prices suddenly react to the information. Regulated markets also have higher chances of insider information compared to forex markets.

A variety of pairs to trade

There are eight major currencies traded in the forex market, and they result in 28 major currency pairs that one may choose from. A trader can select any pair and easily switch from one to the other.

Low-capital requirements

A trader can start trading in the forex market with a low amount of initial capital because of the tight spread in relation to pips. In some other markets, one may not be able to trade without a large amount of capital. To ice the low capital cake, forex exchange also has a margin trading and leverage factor.

Technical strategy

Many traders venturing into bonds and equity have to delve deep into the financial and fundamental state of the bonds or share issuer in order to confirm that there are chances of making a profit. However, the forex market, traders do not have to dig too deep, all they need is to study the price charts. Technical analysis of forex market price charts helps the traders identify their entry and exit points. However, they may choose to combine technical and fundamental analysis when selecting a trade.

While fundamental analysis requires one to get detailed background information about the assets of the issuer and the financial health and prospects, Technical analysis requires one to watch the trends and histories of the market, therefore, getting clues on the demands and supply of the currencies.

No insider price manipulation

Many markets such as stock markets and bond markets can be influenced by information held privately by some investors and insiders who have interests in the assets. This is because most of the markets are centralized. Foreign exchange markets are not centralized; therefore, they cannot be easily manipulated by people who have insider information.

In most cases, the only holders who can access insider information in the forex exchange are central bank authorities or government officials, and they are usually under a lot of intense scrutiny from the public and the private sectors. As such, the foreign exchange market is one of the most transparent markets one can trade in.

Few commissions and fees

Traders get charged Pricey commissions and hidden trading fees when dealing with bonds, equities mutual funds and other kinds of instruments. This makes trading very expensive and reduces the profits of the trader. In forex trade, the costs of trading are determined by the bid-ask price only. The spread price is the difference between the bid and the asking price which is clearly published in real time by the brokers. As such, a trader does not have to worry about eliminating breakage overheads. This aspect makes Forex exchange more advantageous to trade in.

Simple tax rules

In many other markets, the traders have to keep track of their trading activities both in the short term and the long term in order to report taxes. However Foreign exchange trading is in most cases subject to a simpler tax rule, therefore, making tax calculations very easy.

Automation

Technology advancements have made it easy for forex traders to trade with utmost ease. The trade has adapted well to automated trading strategies, and with some training, a trader can reap the benefits of the available moves. A trader can set up programming entry, automated trades, limit prices and stop loss before he/she even makes a trade. The trader may also instruct the trading platform to transact when there are certain price movements or market conditions.

When a trader identifies a well revised automated strategy, he/she may have the chance to take advantage of the daily swings in the market without having to put all their efforts in keeping up with the movements in the market.

Suits different trading styles

Trade in the forex market happens at all hours of the day, Monday to Friday, therefore, enabling a trader to work at their own convenience. This schedule is very beneficial especially for short term traders because they take positions over a limited timeframe (a few hours or even a few minutes.). Some traders prefer to trade during off hours. Off hours refer to the times when one trade zone is not so active, and the other is active. For example, when it is daytime in Australia, it is nighttime on the east coast of the United States. If a trader is based in the US, he may trade AUD during the business hours in the US because the prices are quite stable and little development is expected to occur during the off hours for UAD. The traders who prefer off hours trade adopt the strategies of high volumes and low profits because they have a little profit margin. The low-profit margin results from the lack of developments in the particular currency. Off hours traders, therefore, try to compensate the low-profit-margin with high volume trades during the low volatility period. Other trading styles allow the traders to hold positions for a longer time; days to several weeks.

Disadvantages

Although trading may appear easy at first sight, some challenges make it hard for the traders. In some cases, the challenges can have serious adverse effects on the trader.

Volatility

All markets show volatility at one point or another. The forex market is not excluded from volatility. Forex traders are exposed to volatilities at times, and if the effects are negative, the trade will be unprofitable.

Forex can disadvantage small traders

In a day, the foreign exchange market can transact up to but not limited to $5 trillion. That huge amount of transaction is usually done by the main layers such as hedge funds, banks, and other larger institutions. These major players have access to a lot of capital, technology and also information that might give them an upper hand while making decisions; therefore, they are naturally advantaged. To some extent, these major players can influence the movement of prices in the market.

On the other hand, a small trader will have to stay alert and utilize the latest information in the best way possible because the forex market is very fast moving. The reality of small traders being disadvantaged is evident in almost all markets, but the forex exchange market is highly affected.

The forex market is not regularized, and it is dominated by brokers. The fact that there are many brokers makes it hard to have full transparency. A trader is competing against professionals, and he/she may not have a say in how the trade order gets fulfilled. The trader may also not get a good price, and he/she will only have access to the quotes provided by the selected broker. The best course is to deal with the brokers who are under the broker regulators. Although the market is not regulated, the actions of the brokers are.

The complex process of price determination

The rates in the forex markets are determined by multiple factors such as global politics, economic status, among others. Some of these factors can pose challenges in analyzing and quantifying, therefore, a trader can have a hard time drawing reliable conclusions on the trade. To a large extent, forex trading relies on technical indicators (Mathematical calculations based on volume, price or open interest of securities). Technical analysts analyze historical data and use the indicators to predict the price movements in the future. If a trader gets the predictions wrong, he/she will incur losses.

Lighter regulatory protection

Many traders and investors have a list of securities they can choose to trade in, and they prefer to act on trades that are swift and have transparent pricing. For most well-known securities, trading takes place in on formal exchanges constituting of large institutions that set the regulations and are regularized to guarantee an active market, a flow of assets and healthy supply/demand balance.

Foreign exchange market is not centralized and does not have a fixed oversight regulation; therefore, it is an over the counter market. The main challenge with over the counter markets is that the trader will have to conduct a due diligence investigation to confirm the reputation and trading practices of the brokers before opening an account with them. Again, lighter regulatory protection might put the trader at risk because; depending on the country that one is trading in, he/she may have no way of getting compensated if he/she feels that the broker gave unfair treatment.

Fewer residual returns

Some trade instruments such as bonds and stocks have a regular schedule for payment of dividends and interests; therefore, they have an enhanced long-term value. However, foreign exchange trade aims at gaining immediate capital gains from a currency pair when one currency appreciates. Again, the forex exchange can either get or pay interest when a position is held overnight. This varies depending on the country that is issuing the currency.

Summary of the pros and cons of the forex market

To a large extent, the foreign exchange market is accessible, potentially lucrative and flexible. The trading environment is extensive (all over the world), liquid and transparent therefore good for traders. When one takes into account the inherent risks of the trade, he will find that most of them are present in all other markets and trading activities. As such the forex market offers ample opportunities for a trader to succeed if he/she is willing to come to terms with the inherent characteristics and conventions of the currency market.

Chapter 2. Swing Trading

Swing trading is a strategy where you hold your investments for a couple of days to a couple of weeks. Swing trading is possible on all CFD instruments, including stocks, Forex, commodities and even indices. In the Forex market, swing trading allows traders to benefit from excellent liquidity, enough volatility to get interesting price moves, all within a relatively short time frame. A swing trader generally works on four-hour (H4) and daily (D1) charts, and may use a combination of fundamental analysis and technical analysis to guide trading decisions. Whether there is a long-term trend, or whether the market is largely range-bound, doesn't really matter. A Forex swing trader is not going to hold on to a position long enough for it to count significantly. Instead, volatility is the key for swing traders. The more volatile the market is, the greater the number of short-term price movements, and this creates more opportunities for swing trading.

When you swing trade, you take time to investigate the trend. For example, you think of trading the Euro/American dollar (EUR/USD) pair. Make sure this pair is a good investment. So you take a few days to a week and analyze the history of the Euro and American dollar. You notice it's one of the most popular pairs on the forex market.

Swing traders will have several trades in their portfolio. Many full-time swing traders will make at least one trade throughout their day, if not more. However, they don't trade as often as a day trader or a scalper. However, there are some swing traders who strategize their trades differently. They may only hold a few trades in their portfolio and complete a trade a few times a month. But when they make a trade, they often receive a large profit. The number of trades you hold in your portfolio will depend on how much time you put toward your trading and if you have a broker who helps manage your account.

When it comes to analyzing charts, swing traders generally focus on daily and weekly charts. Of course, you are able to look as far back as you want to gain the best idea for trading. However, you also need to understand that no matter how hard you try, you can't tell the future. You use charts in order to gain the best idea. You always need to remember the forex market is fluid.

One of the biggest risks with forex swing day trading is holding trades for a long time. Even though the forex market doesn't close like the stock market, forex day traders carry overnight risks as they are not there to watch their portfolio. You always need to keep in mind a lot of change that can happen when you are away from your trades. For example, the biggest overnight risk for forex traders will happen during the weekend when the market is closed. This is when you will find your biggest price gaps, which can cause you to lose a lot of your capital. While there can be price gaps overnight during the week, they are usually not as large and are more manageable.

Is Swing Trading Right for You?

If you are willing to take an overnight risk, then swing trading might be for you. This risk can cause many people to become anxious when they wake up in the morning, especially when they first start investing. Placing your money into your account with the knowledge that the future is never really set can be stressful for any beginner. Before you start, you need to be comfortable with the overnight risk.

If you find researching and analyzing daily and weekly reports to be fun and exciting, you will want to look into swing trading. You need to have a good understanding of how to read these reports and take time to make notes so you can make the best decisions possible when it comes to buying and selling your investments.

If you have the time to put toward the research, then you will want to look into swing trading. While you don't have to be a full-time trader, you will want to ensure you set up a schedule and follow through. Many people will struggle with this, especially if they don't have the self-discipline to focus on the market instead of distractions. If you want to go into swing trading but know you lack self-discipline, take time to learn a few self-discipline techniques. Make this part of your beginner's research.

How to Apply Swing Trading?

One of the main points in applying swing trading is to find the right trades. This is going to take time and patience. Many people focus on common currency pairs at the beginning, such as the US dollar/euro (USD/EUR) or US dollar/Canadian dollar (USD/CAD).

Because you need to hold your trades longer than a day, you need to use the stop-loss technique. Through your money management, you will be able to identify when you should exit a trade in order to gain your maximum profit.

Strategies to Use

There are several strategies you can use when applying swing trading in the forex market.

Trend Following

One of the most popular swing-trading strategies is trend following. In fact, this strategy will be used in conjunction with every strategy because you will always need to know how to read the trend lines in charts.

There are several parts to trend following. The first part is knowing the moving averages, which will be shown as red and blue lines in the trading charts. Moving averages will help you find the lines of support and resistance. There are two types of moving averages. The first type is the exponential moving average (EMA). This type gives the most recent points a greater significance. The second type is the simple moving average (SMA), which places significance on all of the prices equally (Lioudis, 2019).

You will also want to pay attention to the candlestick charts as they will tell you the price information. In a candlestick chart, you will be able to quickly notice when the closing rate is lower than the opening rate through to colors of the candlestick. For example, when the opening rate is higher, the candlestick is going to be filled in. When the closing rate is higher, the candlestick is going to be clear. These charts will also explain which direction the price is heading, whether it is in an upward trend or downward trend. You will also be able to notice any pattern within the candlestick trend. For example, you might notice the pattern declines during a certain part of the month and then continues to climb back up.

The second part is making sure you place the right amount of money within your trade. If you place too much money in your account, you can end up with a large capital loss. However, if you don't place enough, you won't reach the full benefits of the trade. It's a challenge to find the right amount; however, with research and help from your broker or financial adviser, you will find this amount.

Finally, you always want to understand the risk of every trade. As you do your research, note the risk, and then look at your trading plan. If your plan doesn't match up with the risk, move on to the next trade.

Options

If you are looking at increasing a return on trade through borrowed money, which is leverage, you can use the options strategy. This strategy can be tricky for a beginner because you have to ensure you are going to receive a profit. The options strategy helps limit your risk because you can set up a time when you buy and sell a position. However, it also locks you in with an agreement. This means that you cannot exit out of a trade if something goes wrong. You have to wait until the agreed-upon time.

In order to limit your risk as much as possible, you want to ensure you have thoroughly researched the currency pair. Notice all the details about the trend lines for the last few weeks. In fact, it might help you to look at the last couple of months as you will get a better idea. From there, you can set up a time to execute the trade that matches the patterns of the charts.

Pros and Cons of Swing Trading

Pros

- It can be more exciting than positions trading.
- It's not as stressful as day trading or scalping.
- You can turn swing trading into a full-time or part-time job.
- You can make huge profits in a short period.

- You don't need to spend all your time as a trader in front of your monitor because the trades will last for a couple of days to a few weeks.
- You will have more time to work on research.
- Swing trading is a great strategy to use when it comes to simulation trading, which is getting real trade experience without using actual money.

Cons

- Swing trading brings overnight risk.
- You won't be able to gain higher profits by holding on to a position for months or years.
- It takes longer to receive a return than day trading or scalping trading.
- Swing trading tends to have less leverage than day trading.

Tips for Beginners

Ensure You Have Your Daily Schedule Set

When you start to focus on trading full-time, you want to ensure you have your daily schedule set and you have enough self-discipline to follow it. For example, the forex market is open 24 hours a day, Monday through Friday and is closed on the weekends. Therefore, you need to set up a time you want to focus on the market. You might decide to be a night trader, which is often quieter or a day trader. Whether you choose night or day, you will want to set your hours. For example, a day forex trader might work from 9:00 a.m. to 4:00 p.m. as this is the busiest time for the forex market.

You also want to ensure you have set enough time aside to read the news, get any morning reports accomplished, and anything else. At the same time, you want to create a closing routine, such as saving your daily reports, making notes on them, writing in a journal, or anything else to end the day or prepare for the next day.

Join an Online Community

There are many communities you can join online for any type of trading. These communities can give you support and help you understand the world of trading. While some communities can be found on social media sites such as Facebook, most of the forums are through various web pages. They are also managed by experienced traders who have years and decades of experience.

Some of the most popular online forums are Elite Swing Trading, Trading Heroes, and Morpheus Trading Group. All these sites have their own forum where you can converse with other traders from all backgrounds and levels of expertise. They also have other information about trading. In fact, some sites will host educational opportunities.

Your Direction Should Align with the Market

Don't get into the trading business thinking that all your research is going to happen at the beginning. Know that you will continue your research. In fact, expect to perform research every day you sit at your desk. This will help ensure that the direction you are going and the pairs you are trading align with the market. This will give you the best profits and make you a successful swing trader.

Swing exchanging is an exchanging style in which stocks, products or files are purchased or sold by a trader inside a time of one to four days. A definitive point of swing trader is to make profits by riding on the direction of the significant market trends. The traders plan to discover this unique capability of the stocks that move in an extremely brief timeframe and make profits by trading in them. He utilizes various methodologies that assistance he identifies this trend and discovers the high likelihood trades. He thinks about market examples and makes utilization of market indicators that empower him to achieve the objective of a beneficial trade.

Swing trading procedure can be utilized in any market yet it is most well known in stocks. There are two noteworthy propensities that a trader needs to search for on the off chance that he needs to bargain in stocks. Right off the bat, the capital ought to tend to trend. Stocks demonstrate a sporadic movement now and again, and there is no clarification of its action in that specific style. Swing trader must trade in such stocks that trends and not the one that moves sideways.

The swing trader presently can make sure of the kind of stocks he will trade in. Be that as it may, the other most essential component is the trend. Before the trader puts any bias, he makes beyond any doubt that he moves in the direction of the pattern and not against it.

There are specific methods accessible for the trader to affirm and check about the trends. The most critical among them is the trend indicator. It is the most famous method to identify trends in the market. The two commonly utilized indicators are the Relative Strength Index and Moving midpoints. The other method to check the trend is The Price Action Trend. This method is broadly utilized by the individuals who get a kick out of the chance to trade without using indicators. This technique is a champion among the most robust and most established ways to identify trends. Rotate Point Trend is one more solid method to identify trends by utilizing turn focuses.

Consequently, there are an extensive variety of ways that can genuinely help a swing trading business to recognize the patterns. They most commonly use these three methods. They are particularly helpful for the newcomers as they should recollect that trend is everything in swing trading.

Swing trading is one of the ways in which you can earn a living. The surest way of making it big is mastering your skill such as computer programming for information technologists. The more skilled you are in trading, the more your compensation. The advantage of mastering a skill is that you will be safe and sure regarding income. Swing trading is one of the best ways you can use to make a lot of money. It provides you with the prospect of generating money based on the quality of the trades you open. The more experienced you are at trading, the higher your potential of making huge gains. Forex markets move in different patterns that can be categorized into two groups:

- Consolidating
- Trending

A market is said to be trending when the price puts in greater lows and highs in an uptrend and does the opposite for a downward movement. The thrust in the major direction is known as an impulse motion, and a recovery in price against the direction of the impulse is called a price correction. The word "move" can be substituted by the word "swing." The diagram below shows a price movement or swing in a trending market.

Swing trading is the practice of making profits from a short-term movement of prices of securities. In swing trading, trades are left open for a few days to a few weeks. Sometimes they can be left open for a maximum of one or two months. Swing traders can be institutions such as hedge funds or individuals. They rarely invest 100 percent in the market at any time, but they wait for low-risk trading opportunities in the market and ensure they make a lot of money from the opportunity. When the market is riding high, they open many buy positions. When the market is weak, they open sell positions or short more often than they buy. When the market is calm (prices not changing much), they do not open any trades.

Advantages of Swing Trading

Swing trading has many merits over other trading styles such as day trading.
It requires just a few minutes every day to manage your open trades, unlike day trading.
Swing trading offers larger targets and plenty of time to open trades.
You tend to have the option of a larger stop loss placement meaning that swing trades are less sensitive to small changes in price (whipsaw) that happens most of the time we have news announcements or during the market day.

Although many people view volatility as a bad aspect because it represents a negative side of the trade that is; the uncertainty and risk, some traders look at it as a plus for making profits. Market players can find volatility in the market very attractive because it also indicates the possibility of making profits. The chances of reaping massive profits on account of volatility are very high, especially for day traders. However, volatility may not work well for long term traders who prefer to buy and hold.

It is important to note that volatility does not indicate the direction of the market. It, however, indicates the level of moves (fluctuations) of an exchange rate. A currency that has high volatility indicates that there are high chances of an increase or a decrease. A currency that has lower volatility indicates lower chances of an increase or a decrease. One example of low volatility is a savings account whereby the investor does not have chances of losing 50 percent of the money, but neither does he have chances of getting 50 percent profit

No one currency stays in high volatility or low volatility forever; there are some time frames when the price of a currency rises and falls so quickly (highly volatile) while other times they seem to be stagnant (less volatile.).

There are two general types of volatility namely historical volatility and expected volatility. One can define Historical volatility as statistical volatility, and it measures the price fluctuations over a particular time. Expected volatility identifies the balance between demand and supply of a currency and uses this to determine the future.

Traders regard volatility as one of the most crucial pieces of information that indicate if the trader should enter or exit a currency position. There are different indicators used to appraise the volatility, and they include Commodity Chanel Index, Bollinger Bands, and Average True Range. All the indicators are comprehensively integrated into most of the trading platforms. The Relative Volatility Index is also another important indicator that reflects the direction that the price volatility is following. The main characteristic of the Relative Volatility Index is that it confirms the RSI, MACD, Stochastic and other Forex oscillators' signals without being repetitive. The Relative Volatility Index serves as a very helpful verification tool because it is drawn from the dynamics of data in the market that are left out by other indicators. When used as a strainer for independent variables, the Relative Volatility index can define the strength of the market trend while measuring up the volatility rather than price.

Foreign exchange traders have for a long time chosen the currency pairs they want to invest in based on the classical analysis of risk and return. Again, the risks and returns are assessed in separate moments and the best-case scenario, for a certain time series. In real trade, the prices of the currencies change constantly and at different speeds that is, sometimes quickly and other times slowly. As such, a trader should pay a lot of attention to volatility because it measures the price range of currencies in the past, the present and the future comprehensively. Consequently, a trader is able to estimate the potential return and the expected risk of an investment.

Taking advantage of volatility

Besides the fact that the foreign exchange market is the largest and one of the most liquid markets, it is also very volatile. Remember that volatility indicates the rises and falls of prices in the markets. The prices of currencies in the forex market can be highly volatile or less volatile depending on the economic conditions. One of the reasons that traders find the forex trade very attractive is the volatility. It offers traders more chances of making quick and huge profits, but one should remember that it also increases the chances of loss. In other words, it is a double-edged sword.

When one observes the forex market closely, he/she will realize that the core of the market movement is volatility. Although geopolitical tensions, market movements, and other factors are the ultimate movers of the markets, volatility rides on the backs of all other factors.

Remember that volatility is classified into two, Historical and expected/ implied. There are a number of things that a trader should do in order to survive the volatile market environment. First, the trader should have the possibility to change his/her leverage with ease. Traders use leverage to make large profits when using limited funds. However, this also increases the chances of making extensive losses. Secondly, a trader should not place all his/her trading capital in a single pair currency because the uncertainty is high in the volatile markets. The outcomes are very uncertain compared to normal market conditions. Therefore, a trader should diversify. Thirdly, a trader should watch out when there are big changes in the forex market and trade smaller. In cases of big movements, a trader should adjust his/her targeted prices. Fourthly, a trader should have the big picture in mind and also monitor trends in larger timeframes. It is even better if the trader can use several timeframes. Finally, the trader should be patient and stay committed to his/her trading plan. Sometimes trading also means staying out of the market; therefore if a trader is too unsure of what to do, he/she should stay out of the trade.

Technical indicators of volatility

Bollinger Bands

Bollinger band indicator was invented by John Bollinger in the 1980s, and it is used to gauge the volatility of a market and to spot the times when prices are about to reverse. They are based on a moving average and normally take into account a 20-period timeframe plotted on a graph. The bands are then formed with standard deviations (two curves plotted above and below the moving average). The theory states that if the deviation of prices indicates a normal distribution, then 95 percent of the fluctuations should fall between the two standard deviations (between the two bands). Any fluctuations that fall outside the standard deviation bands should indicate increased volatility and prices are likely to fall back to their average.

Average True Range

The average true Range indicates the average trading range for a particular period of time. A trading range is defined as that time when a currency trades between consistent low and high prices for a certain timeframe. In a trading range, the upper trading range provides price resistance while that at the bottom typically provides the support. In the case of forex trade, the predetermined amount of time is 14 period. When the Average true range decreases, it indicates a decrease in volatility. The vice versa is true.

Average Directional Index

The Average Directional Index indicates the length of each trend based on the lows and the highs over a particular timeframe. In forex trade, the time frame is usually 14 periods. The indicator is plotted as one line below the chart, and the values range between 0 and 100. When the line is above the twenty to twenty-five levels, then that indicates that a trend is beginning no matter the direction. When the trend becomes stronger, it indicates that there is increased volatility.

Technical Analysis

Technical analysis is as important as fundamental analysis, especially when it comes to swing trading. However, you could view technical analysis as the more serious of the two types of analysis. Instead of just looking at the basics of the company and the fundamental variables which focus on your potential stock's company, you will focus more on the technical side of your stock when you look at technical analysis.

By definition, technical analysis is measuring the historical trends of the stock. Because many people feel that technical analysis is trickier than fundamental analysis, it might be wise to do more research about the topic before you start analyzing any stocks. There are a few online classes and books that are available for you, if you feel the need to become well educated on technical analysis.

One of the biggest factors to remember when you are focusing on technical analysis is you want to make sure to study every detail of your stock's history. You want to make sure you understand the trend, have made any notes you needed to, and that you believe you see the trend giving you the best profit before you decide to take on the stock. Technical analysis is going to take time and patience. However, you also don't want to spend too much time trying to decide if you want to take on a specific stock or not. This is a special time balance that you will figure out once have opened your account and on your way to trading stocks.

What You Will Study Through Technical Analysis

There are several details of the stock's history that you will look at when you are focusing on the technical analysis part of your trading schedule. This is something that you will do with every stock as it will help you decide if this stock is going to be worth your energy and time.

In order to give you a better view of what type of things you will look for, I will briefly discuss them below.

Study of Charts

Of course, one of the main pieces of the stock you will look at are the historical charts. These charts will give you some of the most detailed information that will help you make the best decision possible for your swing trading journey.

One of the most common charts are known as candlestick charts. These charts received this name because they are shaped like a candlestick. On top of that, the information you will find in the chart is designed through the candlestick. There are two main reasons why traders like candlestick charts so much. First, these charts are fairly easy to read and understand. Not only do they give you the information you need to know but they will also show off colors. The second reason is because these charts are known to give you an indication that the trend is about to change. For many people, this is extremely helpful because it decreases the amount of research that you need to do. However, there are other people that still say you should always perform your own research to make sure that the candlestick chart is correct on its assumption.

In general, the candlestick chart will tell you what the opening price was for the stock, the highest price, the lowest price, and the closing price. By getting these prices, you will start to analyze the chart to see what type of trend this stock is following. By looking at the history of the stock, you can start to get a sense of what the average prices are throughout the day. On top of this, you will also be able to get a sense of how much the stock tends to jump up and down during the day. On top of this, the candlestick chart will change colors in the center, depending on if the stock made a profit that day between the opening and closing price.

Of course, you will want to do this type of analysis for any chart that you come across, whether it is a line or pie chart. While each chart will look a bit different, they will all have the same valuable information within them. They will all tell you what the prices were throughout the day. However, not all of the charts will give you a prediction to what the trend will be doing next.

Volume

Another major part of technical analysis is the volume of a stock (lot or currency in the Forex market). The reasons why the volume is so important is because you will be able to get a sense of the intensity of the currency's movement in price. What this means is you will be able to take a certain amount of time, whether it is a few hours or a few months and get an idea of how many lots were traded during this time. Of course, the more lots that you find are traded, the better the currency is for trading. Lots tend to reach high volume for many reasons. For example, they could be considered one of the more popular trading currencies on the market. Another reason is because higher volume tends to mean a better profit. Think about it – people don't often take on trades where they are less likely to make a profit. Therefore, if the volume is high you know that most traders have found this currency to be successful.

Analyzing the Trend Line

I have already discussed a lot of information about trend lines in this book. By now, you should know that it is one of the main factors that will help you determine the success rate of a currency and whether you want to take on this currency or not. However, I feel it is important to mention that whenever you are analyzing a trend line, you are using technical analysis. You are not only analyzing what the trend line has done the previous day or the last couple of days, but you are most likely looking at the trend line over a period of months. The farther back you go, the more you will be able to learn details about the currency trends.

What is a Lot in Forex Trading?

In the past and even presently in MT4, spot forex is traded in specific amounts called lots. A lot in forex trading is basically the pre-defined number of currency units you will buy or sell when entering a trade.

This table will help you understand the different types of lot available in forex trading.

LOT NAME	NUMBER OF UNITS	MT4 NOTATION	PIP VALUE $
Standard	100,000	1 Lot	$10
Mini	10,000	0.1 Lot	$1

Micro	1,000	0.01 Lot	$0.1
Nano	100	0.001 Lot	$0.01

The size of a standard lot in forex trading means 100k units of your account currency. That's a $100,000 trade if you are trading in dollars.

If you have a dollar-based account, then the average pip value of a forex standard lot is approximately $10 per pip. That means if you are trading a standard lot, then a 10 pip movement in the market will give you a $100 profit/loss depending on the direction of movement.

It is recommended to trade in forex standard lot size only if you have $25,000 or more in your trading account.

Beginners should only trade Nano or Micro lots.

Technical Analysis - Charting Basics

Technical analysis is measuring the historical trends of the currency. Because many people feel that technical analysis is trickier than fundamental analysis, it might be wise to do more research about the topic before you start analyzing any stocks or currencies. There are a few online classes and books that are available for you, if you feel the need to become well educated on technical analysis.

One of the biggest factors to remember when you are focusing on technical analysis is you want to make sure to study every detail of your currencies' history. You want to make sure you understand the trend, have made any notes you needed to, and that you believe you see the trend giving you the best profit before you decide to take on the currency pair. Technical analysis is going to take time and patience. However, you also don't want to spend too much time trying to decide if you want to take on a specific lot or not. This is a special time balance that you will figure out once have opened your account and on your way to trading currencies.

In essence, swing trading is all about price trends and momentum. As more and more traders make consistently superior trading profits using swing trading, it continues to grow in popularity among traders. And when it comes to technical analysis for swing trading, swing charts have become swing traders' weapons of choice.

Swing Charting

Keeping the two price turning points in mind, swing charting involves taking or closing positions using such points as triggers or signals for doing so:

- An up day following a down day turning point is a signal or trigger to buy a financial security; and
- A down day following an up day turning point is a signal or trigger to sell a financial security.
- That's how simple using a swing chart is. Traders can use swing charts for several purposes, such as:
- Seeing the general trend of specific markets or financial securities in a very easy and practical way, sans the "distortions" or noises, and by just looking for turning points via the stairs-like patterns or trend lines.
- Taking stop-loss or profit-taking positions via the turning points, i.e., previous selling and buying turning points can act as points of reference for future swing trades.
- Using other advanced but not time-sensitive technical analysis tools like Elliott Waves and the Fibonacci technique, which are considered as leading technical indicators.
- Creating price bands or channels, within which traders can set fairly reliable buying and profit-taking positions.

Swing charting can make it much easier for traders to identify price trends by removing the element of time and price "noise" from the equation. And because it can do so, it can also make it much easier and simpler to consistently make winning swing trades.

Some readers of this book may be well-versed on this topic already while others may be new to trading and charting. This section is critical for new traders because many swing trade strategies are based on graphing price action and reading charts that are readily available online.

Candlesticks

While these early versions of technical analysis and candlestick charts were different from today's version, many of the principles are similar. The type of candlestick charting that traders are familiar with today first appeared sometime after 1850.

Candlesticks do not just represent the price action of a stock a lot or currency pair during a period of time. When these candlesticks are put together in a timeline, they can also be thought of as a window that gives the trader some insight into the overall market sentiment or feeling about a stock a lot's or a currency pair perceived value. Candlesticks convey the majority of the traders' psyche regarding that valuation over the period of time being examined.

The time frame can be 1 minute, 5 minutes, hourly, daily, weekly, or any other period you choose. Typically, with swing trading, traders will commonly look at daily charts or those that cover longer periods of time because your hold time will typically be measured in days or weeks or possibly even longer intervals. From the set of numbers listed above, you can create a candlestick.

Bar Charts

Both charts show the same information and it is a matter of personal preference as to which option you choose to use. Most charting tools will provide you with multiple options regarding chart type, color, time frame, etc. Regardless of which charting style you choose, candlestick and bar chart patterns tell you a great deal about the general trend of a stock and the level of interest between buyers or sellers of that lot, stock or currency pair.

Price Action and Psychology

The presence and actions of undecided traders can put pressure on either the buyers or the sellers depending on which way this group is leaning. These undecided traders could suddenly decide to take a position and make the deals that the others are considering. If the buyers wait too long to decide on a transaction, someone else could beat them to it and drive up the price. The sellers who wait too long for a higher price might be disappointed by other traders who sell at the bid, which drives the price down. Their ongoing awareness of the presence of undecided traders makes the buyers and sellers more willing to trade with each other.

The buyers are buying because they expect that prices will go up. If there are more buyers than sellers, then the result is that buyers are willing to pay higher and higher prices and subsequently will bid on top of each other. When this occurs it is said that the "buyers are in control". They are apprehensive that they will end up paying higher prices if they don't buy now. When undecided traders see the price increase, they may also decide to become buyers, which creates a feeling of urgency among all of the buyers. The price of the lot or currency then starts to accelerate further upward.

The sellers are selling because they expect that prices will go down. When a lot or a currency pair price is dropping it means that the "sellers are in control". The result is that sellers are willing to accept lower and lower prices to get out of their positions. They are concerned that they will end up selling at even lower prices if they miss selling immediately. Undecided traders who are holding the stock see the selling pressure and they decide to sell as well. This added selling creates a sense of urgency among the sellers, causing the lot or currency price to drop faster.

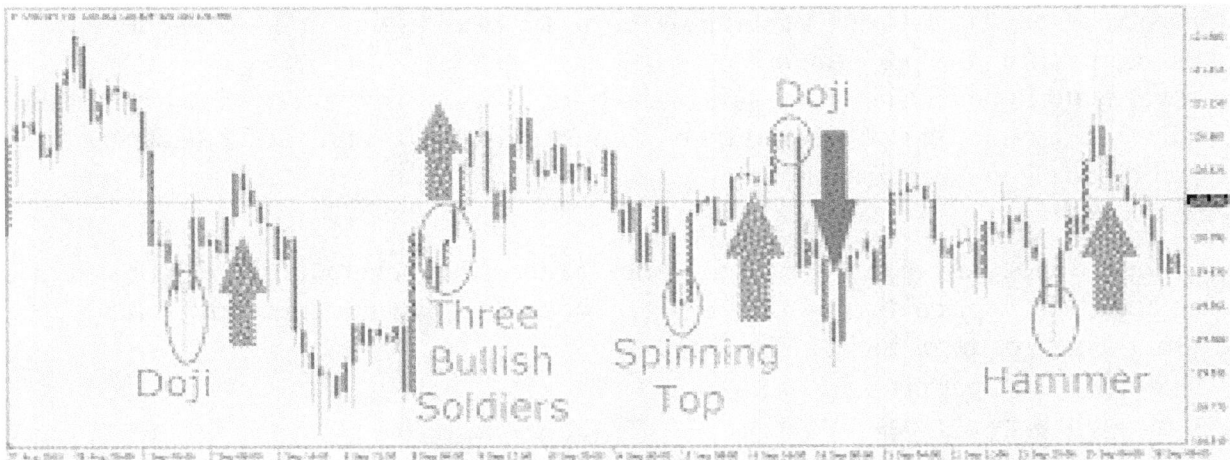

Candlestick Patterns

Basic Bullish and Bearish Candlesticks

A seasoned swing trader will also confirm the bullish move by checking the volume (the number of lots being traded during that time period). Increasing volume relative to previous periods will confirm that the trend is strong. The volume of lots traded is represented by a bar located under the candlestick. The height of the bar is proportional to the number of lots traded.

The candlestick on the right is more bullish in comparison to the one on the left. The figure also shows the volume bars underneath the candlesticks with the tall bar representing a larger number of lots traded in comparison to the smaller bar.

As with bullish candlesticks, a seasoned trader will again check the number of lots traded in the period to see if during the selling the volume was increasing relative to previous periods. This is another confirmation that the sellers are firmly in control of the price movement.

The candlestick on the right is more bearish compared to the one on the left. The figure also shows the volume bars underneath the candlesticks with the tall bar representing a larger number of lots traded in comparison to the smaller bar.

By learning to read these candlesticks and the patterns that they generate over a period of time, you will begin to understand which group of traders is in control of the price action. Is there overall buying pressure pushing the currency price higher or are the sellers in control and pushing the price lower?

You never want to be on the wrong side of the trade. This is why you need to learn how to read candlesticks or bar charts and then be constantly interpreting and reassessing the price action while you are in a trade.

Reversal Candles

In fact, there are dozens of different candlestick patterns but several are fairly consistent in predicting future price direction, especially when used in conjunction with other indicators. These patterns include the following:

- engulfing pattern
- doji: harami cross
- doji: gravestone and dragonfly

Let's examine the characteristics of each of these patterns in more detail.

Engulfing Pattern

One of these popular trading pattern setups is referred to as an engulfing candle. This engulfing candle pattern illustrates a potential change in control between the buyers and sellers. The engulfing pattern can either be bullish or bearish, which means either the buyers are taking control (bullish) or the sellers are taking control (bearish).

The trading volume is used to confirm a change in control with this indicator usually being displayed at the bottom of a chart as a bar. The short candle has lower volume indicating that the buying or selling action is getting exhausted. The longer reversing candle will have a higher volume of trades, which indicates that control has changed hands and there is likely a decisive shift in the direction of the stock price.

In addition, the chart shows a harami cross, which also indicates a potential change in stock price direction.

These engulfing candlesticks can be bearish or bullish. A bullish engulfing candlestick suggests that the bulls have taken control of the price action. Leading up to the engulfing candlestick it was the bears who would have had control of the stock, keeping the price action in a downtrend. The bullish engulfing candlestick accompanied by a spike in volume indicates either a large new interest in owning the stock or possibly the covering of short positions held by traders.

It is important to get into a reversal trade early to ensure that you have the best possible risk to reward ratio. You should look at your chart to identify areas of resistance or support in the currency or market. Some traders might set the stop out price even higher, at the low of the previous candlestick that was engulfed.

Once you know your stop out price level and potential entry price, you can then determine your potential reward by looking at where you would expect to sell. You now have enough information to calculate your risk to reward ratio. If there is at least 2 times more reward compared to risk, it could be a good setup to examine more closely for an entry.

You can also try to assess if there have been some fundamental factors behind a possible reversal. Look for news or other events that might be causing a reversal in order to confirm the trade you are considering.

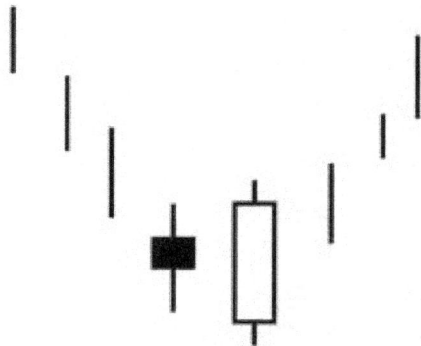

Bullish Engulfing   **Bearish Engulfing**

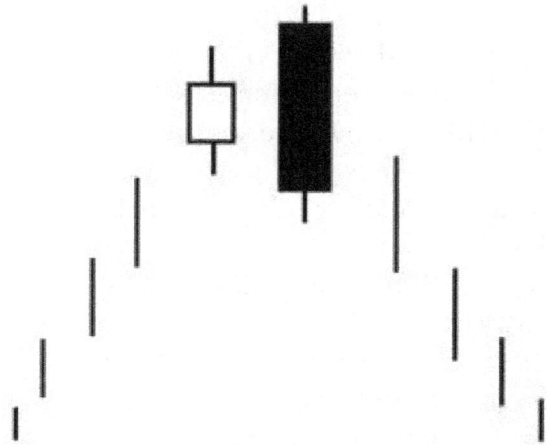

Doji – Harami Cross

One particular type of doji that shows a potential reversal in price action is called the *Harami cross*. The key to reading this pattern is to look for the trading volume confirmation. You should see strong volume on the preceding days followed by a drop in volume with shorter tails on the final Harami cross candlestick. This change in volume and price action usually indicates a shift in traders' confidence on the continued direction of the currency price.

You can see how a Harami cross appeared just before an engulfing candle in the chart of TZA, indicating the price was ready to reverse and move higher. The engulfing candle confirmed this signal and shows how this indicator can be used in combination with other indicators.

Doji – Gravestone and Dragonfly

The gravestone Doji can be found at the end of an uptrend as shown on the left side of the figure. The long upper tail suggests that the bulls took control early but later in the period it was the bears who were in control, pushing the price back down to the open.

The dragonfly Doji is the opposite of the gravestone in that it is the bears who start out in control of the price by pushing it lower at the open. As the period continues, the bulls take control of the price movement, returning the price back to the open.

Traders should also look at the volume of shares traded with the Doji and compare that volume to the previous period – ideally the volume will be equal to or larger during the period that the Doji occurred.

Doji patterns can be traded in a similar way as to how you would trade an engulfing candle. The first objective is to get in as early as possible when you recognize the pattern appearing. For example, on a *dragonfly Doji*, a swing trader could go long with their stop at the bottom of the tail. A tighter stop for a more conservative trader would be about 50% of the tail.

Again, you should check other indicators to get some confirmation that a potential reversal in price action is happening. Also, you should assess if there have been some fundamental factors behind a possible reversal.

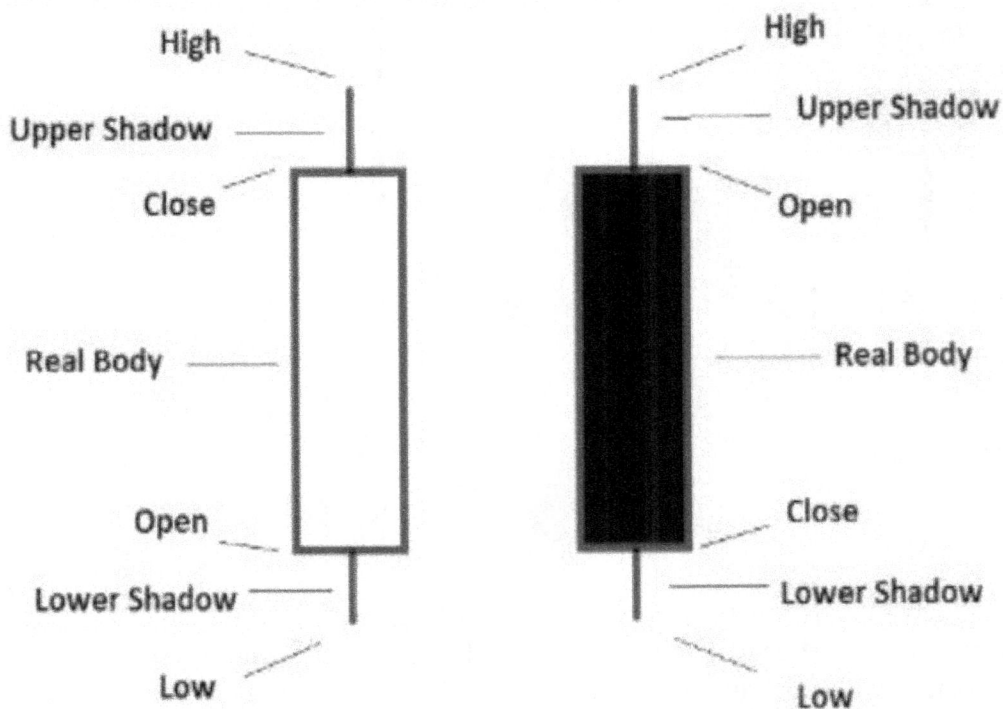

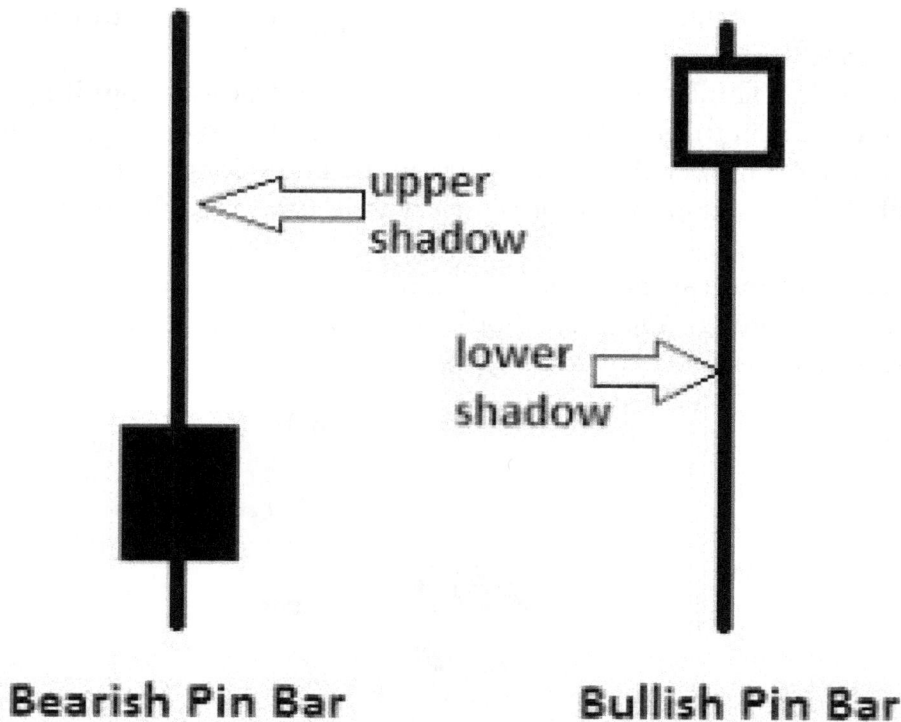

Bearish Pin Bar **Bullish Pin Bar**

Gaps

Gapping price action normally occurs between trading sessions. The size of the gap is often very small but at other times it can be very large. Larger gaps are usually caused by some new information that has come to light, which affects the sentiment of the traders and investors toward the currency. It could be negative news such as reduced economic growth or it could be good news such as the announcement of record industrial production. After a gap has occurred, 1 of 3 things will happen:

Gap and Go

The gap and go happens when it takes several days for the market to settle on a new valuation for the currency. This usually happens after a major announcement or event. Overly exuberant buying or selling will drive valuations to such extremes that an eventual pullback will occur.

These types of scenarios will likely play out on extremely good news or in markets that are very bullish or bearish in sentiment. For currencies, lots or stocks gapping higher, if there is a high number of traders holding short positions (over 20% of lots are shorted for example), then panic covering of these short positions creates additional buying that drives the price even higher.

Gap and Consolidate

Some gaps are 1-day events and all of the news gets priced into the currency in the session immediately following the event. After that, the stock's price will move sideways with a bit of up and down action as investors take profits or losses and new investors come in to take new positions. After a period of sideways consolidating price action, the price will start to move higher or lower. The direction the currency goes after consolidation depends considerably on the event and the overall market direction.
If the news was good but the overall market is trending lower, then eventually the market direction may override the event and take the lot's price lower. If the news has long-term implications for the currency (either positive or negative), the currency will likely continue to move in the direction of the gap after consolidation.

Gap and Fill

Some gaps are not sustainable. Traders and investors will take profits in the gap and it is possible that short sellers will see an opportunity to sell high and buy low. Long traders will sell into a pop up in price and the short uptrend will reverse with the stock "filling the gap".
For a swing trader, gaps can be difficult to trade after they have already happened. Gaps can result in overreactions to some news and those overreactions can last a day or they can last for several days. In an uptrending market, a swing trader can take a position during the first day of the gap up. They could take a position near the end of the day if the currency continues to trend higher and closes out the day close to or at the high. There is a good chance under this scenario (a strong market and a strong currency price action) that the price will gap up again on the following day.
Another way to play gaps is to use the gap and fill principle. Often the points where a currency gapped higher or lower become, respectively, levels of resistance or support. This is where it opened on the first gap up day. These levels are often respected and traded by market participants, but once it broke that support level, the price continued to drop back to where it started its journey higher. Knowing where there will likely be levels of resistance and support, a swing trader can make trades based on this principle regarding these levels.

Trading news is harder than it may sound. You have to take into account the reported consensus figure, but also the whisper numbers (the unofficial and unpublished forecasts) and any revisions to previous reports. Furthermore, some releases are more important than others; in terms of both the significance of the country releasing the data and the importance of the release in relation to the other pieces of data being released at the same time.

When Are Key News Releases?
Here are the approximate times (Eastern Time) of the most important economic releases for each of the following countries. These are also the times that players in the forex market should pay extra attention to the markets, especially when trading based on news releases.

Country	Currency	Time (EST)
U.S.	USD	8:30 to 10 a.m.
Japan	JPY	6:50 to 11:30 p.m.
Canada	CAD	7 to 8:30 a.m.
U.K.	GBP	2 to 4:30 a.m.
Italy	EUR	3:45 to 5 a.m.
Germany	EUR	2 to 6 a.m.
France	EUR	2:45 to 4 a.m.
Switzerland	CHF	1:45 to 5:30 a.m.
New Zealand	NZD	4:45 to 9 p.m.
Australia	AUD	5:30 to 7:30 p.m.

What Are the Key Releases?
Generally speaking, the most important information relates to changes in interest rates, inflation, and economic growth, like retail sales, manufacturing, and industrial production:

1. Interest rate decisions
2. Retail sales
3. Inflation (consumer price or producer price)
4. Unemployment
5. Industrial production
6. Business sentiment surveys
7. Consumer confidence surveys
8. Trade balance
9. Manufacturing sector surveys

The relative importance of these releases may change depending on the current state of the economy. At times unemployment may be more important than trade or interest rate decisions. It is therefore important to keep on top of what the market is focusing on in a given moment.

The Different Types of Indicators in the Volume Price Chart

These indicators always follow specific movement criteria where some of them may be of trending markets and others of the range-bound market. Trend marketing looks like they are moving in one direction, whereas a range one seems like a sideways one that runs in a specific range.

The first indicator is the **Relative Strength Index (RSI)**. This indicator compares the magnitude of overbought and oversold conditions on the market. When this scale reads a higher peak, it means the currencies are overbought, and when it leads a low level, it means the currencies were oversold. Investors using the scale should be aware that the significant drop and rise effects can create a false impression in analyzing the trend.

The **Moving Average Convergence Divergence (MACD)** is another indicator. It illustrates the two exponential averages that measure the distances between the moving trends. Convergence means objects are close to each their while divergence shows they are far away from each other. There is a centerline passing along the exponential averages which shows. It is plotted to show when the proportions are equal and when they are crossing on each other. Traders will always target where the MACD is farther away that shows a higher momentum. At this point in time, you are likely to immerse a good return of investments that you are trading.

Let's take a look at this indicator in more detail.

Most trading platforms will come equipped with a MACD indicator that you can simply apply to your chart and begin your analysis. To better understand how the indicator works, we must know what data is being input into the algorithm.

We begin by subtracting the currency pair's 26 day Exponential Moving Average (26 EMA) from the 12 day Exponential Moving Average (12 EMA).

The next step is to plot a 9 day Simple Moving Average (9 SMA) over the top of our MACD signal on the currency pair chart.

Using the MACD indicator to find your entry can be done in various ways. We can, for example, look for the MACD signal line to move above the 9 day SMA. This is a BULLISH sign and indicates a BUY signal of the currency pair. When the MACD signal line crosses below the 9 day SMA, we take this as a BEARISH sign and would look for a SHORT position.

Another method used to extrapolate signals from the MACD is when the underlying currency pair price (9 day SMA) diverges from the MACD signal. This can indicate the end of the current trend, or an imminent reversal of price action. If the MACD signal moves too far above the 9 day SMA, the currency pair may be OVERBOUGHT and a correction is likely to take place.

Bollinger band indicator is used to measure the standard deviations of a simple moving average of the scales. You can consider it an on-chart volatility indicator. During extensive volatile periods, the bands widen and stretch away from each other. At lower volatile, the groups move close to each other and the bands contracts. The indicator includes a standard 20-period Simple Moving Average which could be used to set entry and exit points of trades.

The super trend indicator measures the trend direction. It may not be one of the most used indicators but it is certainly a useful one since it basically tells you the current trend for any forex pair (and in any given time frame) that you wish to look at. The super trend indicator broadly moves in line with the underlying price and will either be green (indicating a bullish trend) or red (indicating a bearish trend). By studying its course and pattern a trader can identify a change of trend, that is when it switches from green to red or vice versa. Even though it's not that helpful on the shorter time frames (too many false moves) it can be invaluable on the longer term charts, especially after a peak or trough in the market or after a long period of sideways consolidation.

This indicator can also be used to determine where to place your stop losses. Placing a stop loss a few pips below the Supertrend indicator if it is currently green, or a few pips above if it is currently red makes a lot of sense.

Analyzing Trading Volume Price Analysis

As Richard Wycoff used to say "you draw from the tape or from your charts, the comparatively few facts which you require for your purpose" these are price movement, intensity of trading, the relationships between price movement and volume, and the time required for all the movements to complete their courses.

The concept is based on the idea that every market is manipulated and, in accepting this fact, we can conclude that market makers, insiders and big operators know where they are taking the market next. All one needs to do to earn a profit, is to understand what the big players are doing and follow them. Buy when they buy, sell when they sell, and stay out when they are not participating.

As we all know there is no central exchange in the spot market. We cannot count how many contracts or indeed the size of contracts traded at any given time ad we have to turn to an alternative measure of volume, which is tick activity.

Within the forex market insiders are the institutional market makers, who create the price spreads, and can see both sides of the market as well as the balance of supply and demand. While they can comfortably hide at the centre of the market, there is one aspect they cannot hide, ad that is volume. They are large in size and their participation (or lack thereof) is very clearly visible when you look at trading volume.

Price moves on large volumes indicate institutional subjects are joining the move.

On the other hand, large moves on low volumes could indicate a trap, with the big players simply moving the price without participation.

In order to use volume price analysis you first have to study in depth the charts and the available information. Try to recognize where the market is heading and spot any anomaly. This preparation phase is essential.

The 11 commandments of swing trading (in a nutshell)

These were originally thought out for stock and commodities but also apply to forex trading.

1. Always align your trade with the overall direction of the market.
You need to identify the longer-term trends to make sure you go with the flow and not against it. Over the years, I've observed that "surprises" such as news announcements, analyst upgrades/ downgrades and earnings hits/misses almost always occur in the direction of the larger trends. Except for very brief periods of time, the long-term trend (as measured by the 30- and 40-week moving averages) and the intermediate trend (as measured by the 10-week moving average) tends to follow the main market trend.

2. Go long strength. Go short weakness.
Once you have identified the overall trend, do not try to fight it. Look for long trades during periods of bullishness. Find appropriate short trades during periods of bearishness

3. Always trade in harmony with the trend one time frame above the one you are trading.
Sure, we all know the cliché- "the trend is your friend." But which trend are people referring to? Use moving averages to be in tune with both the short- and intermediate-term trends, even through as a swing trader you are only trading for the short term.

4. Never trade only on the short-term chart of the swing-trading time frame.
Be sure to synthesize the messages that the weekly, daily and even hourly charts are telling you.
Look at the big picture as if through a telescope as well as the detail using a microscope when you look at charts. Too small a look-back period -- using the microscope only -- can be deceptive and costly.

5. Try to enter the trade near the beginning of the trend, not near the end.
It's never too late to hop on the elevator. If the market is headed from the 100th floor down to the 68th, you can still profitability go short on floor 85. But the quicker you recognize a trend has begun, the more profitable your trade will be and the less risk you will assume.

6. Always apply the rule of "multiple indicators." Do not trade on any one technical tool or concept in isolation.

Highly profitable trades usually occur when all available technical tools give the same message. Candlesticks, volume, moving averages, and indicators such as stochastics and MACD occasionally all align to communicate the same message -- the stock is about to sharply rise or fall. But keep in mind that nothing is 100% accurate, and there is no such thing as "free money."

7. Keep your eye on the ball. Track a consistent group of currency pairs.

As a swing trader, it is easy to jump from one hot currency pair to another. Although it's okay to follow the action, you should also have a core group of currency pairs you track daily and learn the personality of.

8. Always enter a trade with a clear trading plan, the four key elements of which are a target, a limit, a stop loss and an add-on point.

And when you sell, you should immediately determine a re-entry level. Swing trading can lead to impulse buying. Sometimes your impulses can turn out to be profitable, but other times they may not be. Remember: without a clear plan you are merely gambling, not trading

9. Try to put the odds in your favor.

Don't risk a dollar to try to make a dime. On good trades, your chart analysis should always show more upside possibility than downside risk.

10. Be a "techno-fundamentalist" and integrate fundamentals into your technical analysis.

Day traders in positions for 15 minutes to an hour have little need for fundamentals. Swing traders, on the other hand, may often hold positions for several days to several weeks. As such, they can greatly benefit from a better understanding of each currency's fundamental, inherent value.

11. Master the "inner game" of swing trading. Great trading is psychological as well as technical.

Always keep a positive mental attitude about your trading. Do not let bad trades affect you longer than necessary. Learn from your mistakes; regain your emotional and rational balance before you make your next trade.

Chapter 3. Psychological Aspects

Psychology is important in the forex market trading business. People who only rely on available skills and academic knowledge without taking into account the psychological aspects of trading, are prone to make mistakes while trading in the forex market. Overlooking the psychological aspects of trading is one of the greatest mistakes in the business. Because of one's own peculiar psychological bias, the same mistakes are repeated over and over again by different types of forex traders of different nationalities, cultures, and social backgrounds. Making mistakes is what makes us human, but repeating the same mistakes time after time, is far from ideal if you're in the forex trading market.

Another common trait observed among forex traders is fear. This trait creates either flight or fight response in an individual's life. Poor handling of their response to fear, has made many forex traders less successful in the market. It is very difficult to reverse an emotion human beings have felt for millions of years. It is, however, relatively easy to change how we respond to the feeling, by observing how successful traders in the forex market have handled themselves in the past.

Fear has the potential of creating a limiting effect on a person's behavior while trading in the forex market. It can force some to bail out of their position prematurely just as it can push others to "fight to their death". We all have a natural response to fear we must learn to predict, understand and, to a certain degree, to control. Fear isn't good or bad in itself, it's an emotion mankind has developed over millions of years as a response to a dangerous situation. We all react to fear in a slightly different way and in order to be successful traders, we must learn to recognize our automatic reactions, evaluate them and decide whether to accept them or fight them.

Fear can be rational or irrational. Some people's fear is too great or too irrational for them to ever become successful traders. Trading without losses is simply impossible. If you trade there will be losses, it's part of the game, and a good trader accepts it. If you can't accept losses of any kind or form, forex trading is not for you. Losses, in the short term, must be taken into account and limited whenever possible. That is why, before opening a new position you should always calculate and place your stop losses, limits, and have a thorough money management strategy in place, so as not to blow your account if things don't go according to plan.

Good, thorough planning and analysis before entering your positions, setting stop losses and having a battle plan help to keep fear at bay.

Reacting hastily and erratically to an unexpected situation out of fear and by doing so, straying from the original battle plan, can do more damage than the situation itself. A reckless, die-hard, stubborn mentality that doesn't allow one to recognize, in due time, that there has been a radical change of initial conditions on the market and it's time to bail out and curb losses is just as bad.

A person's mind, in very many instances, loves to focus on the short term survival conditions. Traders operating in the foreign exchange market, however, are advised to think and plan critically in the long term. This will allow for the creation of successful a long term plan despite limited losses in the short term.

When an individual operating in the forex market understands trading psychology, he or she has an added advantage in the market. The understanding of human psychology in the forex market helps an individual to eliminate fear while making critical decisions about his or her investments. When an individual is aware of fear in him or her, he or she can get the courage to face the obstacle with correct psychology. The same drill is used in the forex market by successful traders in the business. Successful traders understand market psychology and are not afraid to take high risks. However, these risky operations with low success rates can guarantee the highest earnings once the market storm is over. Understanding market psychology will help beginners in the forex market have the ability to establish control of reasoning and logic. These are the ultimate aims of nearly every single forex trader.

Different Types of Trading Bias

Forex market traders can easily feel confident in their potential to remain collected and calm. This feeling is a common phenomenon before the forex market trading session begins. However, the narrative quickly reverses when the trading session opens. It is very easy for emotions to prevail in a real-life crisis. The same happens when a stock trader deals with real financial decisions challenging his or her investments. Despite these feelings cropping up in real life, people can learn to work through or around hardships and obstacles.

Those who trade in the forex market are not supposed to give in to these feelings. The feelings that forex traders are prone to face include greed, excitement, or fear while trading their investments in the foreign exchange market. If these feelings overcome and cloud their judgment, they are likely to make very costly and irreversible mistakes. Before venturing into the forex market, beginners should thoroughly analyze their character as traders. They are likely to come across one of the following categories of psychological bias in themselves;
· Overconfidence bias; "I am sure the market will head this way"
· Anchoring bias; "this means that probably.."
· Confirmation bias; "this proves I'm also right"
· Loss bias; "I hope commodity prices will come around"
A keen individual who is alert will notice how these biases overlap. Therefore, no matter which angle a person takes, these biases will boil down to creating fear in a trader's mind. The individual biases will be discussed at length to help you identify and be more aware of your emotions.

Overconfidence Bias

The first lesson a beginner in the forex market is supposed to learn is how to train his or her euphoria. It is the first lesson in the trading psychology of forex market. Humans are, most of the time, self-focused creatures. Our ego plays an important role since we always want to validate what we know. These egos tend to go a notch higher to make people prove a point that they are not ordinary people and are better than the average people. Available hints that corroborate with these thoughts do a job of reinforcing our images. It is made possible through a very discrete feeling of self-love.

This feeling makes a cropping problem to forex traders while trading. The traders are prone to being very overconfident, thus succumbing to overconfidence bias. It a very common occurrence for a trader to have a good streak in the forex market and consistently make gains. The trader is predicted to have thought if he or she can't make mistakes or the market will still favor him or her in the future. A trader is discouraged from having these thoughts because it can end up being his or her greatest fall in the trade of forex. An individual in the forex market is supposed to be keen on looking at details of the gains he or she makes. The forex trader is supposed to also go into details in the sessions he or she also makes losses in the market.

Forming the habit of going over your mistakes in detail will help one stay on top of his or her game. People are supposed to make mistakes in life. The same goes for forex market traders who are also bound to make mistakes. Being able to make mistakes and prove oneself wrong is good and will help you in the long run. A person is supposed to be able to accept the fact that making mistakes in life can't be avoided. This is especially true for beginners because everything in life has a learning curve.

Anchoring Bias

The so called anchoring bias is another common occurrence in the forex market. It happens when a trader creates an artificial comfort zone or a psychological benchmark in his mind while performing an analysis of the market situation giving it disproportionate importance during his or her decision-making process. Forex traders with an anchoring bias tend to mistakenly think that the market is somewhat unchanging. For example one can be anchored to the price at which one bought a currency thus becoming fixated with this price even when conditions have changed. Anchoring is a habit created by forex traders that solely rely on what they already know. A trader with this kind of bias has a somewhat closed mindset. He or she fails to take into account the changes the forex market can bring about to his or her investment. Several traders have seen their investments decline because their closed mindset forced them to rely on irrelevant and obsolete information. This bias can make trading very difficult for traders in the forex market.

The anchoring bias manifests itself when a trader holds a single position for a very long time. This because he or she fails to consider other options the forex market can provide. People with this bias are afraid to get out of their comfort zones and explore other options and alternatives. A beginner is supposed to be prepared to try several of the market offers. Anchoring to a single position can make a person rely on outdated information leading to losses.

Confirmation Bias

This form of bias is common among professional forex traders in the market. People with this kind of bias will tend to favor information that confirms their existing beliefs. These investors seek out information that confirms their existing opinions and ignore contrary information that contradicts them, they may distort the value of their investment decisions based on their own biases. Traders with a confirmation bias tend to repeat their mistakes and to keep researching subjects they already know, losing precious time and opportunities. Traders in the forex market are encouraged to trust their instincts and intelligence. This will enable them to create new market strategies improving their profits margins.

Loss Aversion Bias

Some traders and people handle loss worse than others do. Their fear of it worries them more than is realistic or healthy. For this reason their neural pathways need a basic plan – a strategy that factors in losses as predictable and ordinary.

It's helpful to know what types of loss aversion biases you may come across, so they can be identified if and when they appear. If you don't, you will struggle with trading on a basic level. You will also not be very good at it.

Let's take a brief look at four loss aversion biases in order to learn the cognitive basics.

Loss aversion bias no 1 – Status Quo Bias

Status quo bias leaks self-righteousness. It's highly biased towards "going with the flow". While doing very little is often an excellent idea, sometimes it's a very bad one. Especially when events are changing rapidly. Given the demands on day traders to sometimes switch and re-think positions fast, this bias is especially dangerous.

Status quo bias is similar to a buy-and-hold strategy, but the financial world has many overlapping financial fast lanes – currency gusts, economic news plus central bank moves – not to mention swift and unexpected information flows. If you're trading you have to react to these events rapidly.

Status quo bias is not 'safe'. As a matter of fact, often it's very unsafe. Pay attention to everything and be prepared to shift your view.

Second Loss aversion bias type – Disposition Bias

This manifests as a tendency to sell early and hang on (and on and on) to losing stocks. You could term it Wanting-My-Money-Back-it.

It stems from an inability to accept daily mistakes – or that we are simply wrong a number of times

Making mistakes and getting things wrong is normal.

Obviously, to stay in business you need to get enough things right too (and if you can't do this then you should not do forex trading)

This bias has strong links to pride and diffidence. Bear in mind that a currency performance has little relation to its price. You buy on the future value of a commodity, not just the entry ticket price.

The third aversion loss bias is the Prospect Theory Bias; valuing gains and losses in different ways, or a peculiar way of valuing risk.

This theory was originally proposed by Israeli academics Amos Tversky and Daniel Kahneman in the 1970s.

They found that when presented with the same option in two different ways, there's a greater probability of someone picking the option offering greater assurance. In other words, if offered $100, or the chance of $150 but a 10% possibility of losing it, the $100 is generally taken.

Prospect theory is about low risk. If you under-respond to small probabilities, that's still a very risky choice.

Finally the bias that can blow your finances in no time

It's called Martingale. It's not strictly a loss aversion bias but we prefer to consider it such. Martingale bias was born in the gambling dens of eighteenth century and is based on the false premise that sooner or later your luck will change.

The big problem is, you might run out of money by the time your luck changes. Imagine a simple 50-50 coin toss game where losses (or gains) are doubled every time. Flip the coin, lose, double the bet. Flip again, lose, double the bet again. Flip the coin, lose again.. etc. Steer well clear from this kind of bias.

Most traders finally accept they are making trading mistakes related to their psychology. But normally, denial is the first reaction. Over time, people tend to accept the truth. Given the right time, even the naïve traders will learn to accept the truth. Forex trading, however, is not only about trading system and strategies. Mindset plays an important part and the ability to anticipate the forex market has a lot to do with successful trading. You might come across certain websites that advertise robotic trading systems, and mistakenly consider trading psychology useless or absurd. Just remember that those trading systems hardly ever deliver the results they promise. You must study and use your knowledge and skills to trade; only then will you be able to trade successfully. As a beginner, you must try to settle for a simple yet effective strategy, so that you will be able to trade without too much stress or pressure.

Why do you think most naïve traders struggle to make money? You might have seen many people fail in the Forex market. There are many reasons why, but the main reason is the fact of trading without knowing the forex market. Many start trading in the Forex market because they trust the hype fabricated and delivered by the ads you see online, setting unrealistic goals. Some even go as far as quitting their job to trade on the forex market. This is a bad idea for a beginner since you should be sure trading works for you before quitting your job. Others think trading is easy money and continue thinking so no matter how many times you tell them it's not true. These thoughts create tension and stress, making people emotionally unstable and emotionally unstable traders lose money. So, how can a trader develop a winning trading mindset? If you want to develop a trading mindset, you fist of all need to study and do your part. It is important to put the required effort to accomplish what you are looking for. You can't build a winning trading mindset quickly because you have to learn and accept the Forex market as it is. If you try to deny facts about the Forex market, you will not be able to create the right mindset.

You must start developing your trading mindset by handling the risks in trading. First of all, understand that risk management isn't for one trade, preferably it is applicable for all the trades that you enter into. You must make sure to calculate the risk for each trade before you enter into it. When you are managing risks, certain emotions might try to confuse you, but you must not let it happen. Once you start handling your emotions wisely, you will be able to manage trades also. However, the simplest way to control emotion when managing risks is to risk ONLY the amount that you can lose. You must create a mindset that enters into a trade while knowing the probability of losing trade. If you follow this, you will be able to remain in the trading world for a long time. But, it takes practice and patience to create a trading mindset that accepts losses. Also, you must master your trading edge. No matter what trading strategy you are using, you must know it completely to trade successfully.

And, remember, overtrading will never create profits. Instead, overtrading will blow all your hard-earned money. You must trade only when you actually see a profit signal. Don't try to trade just because you feel like trading. Or don't try to guess trade because that doesn't work in Forex trading. If you overtrade, it can be challenging to stop, and you'll become an emotional trader.

If you want to build a trading mindset, you must have an organized mindset. So, basically, when you have an organized mindset, you will think about the trading plan, journal, and much more. You must accept the fact that Forex trading is a business. Hence, don't try to gamble in the market. When you are making trading decisions, you must remain calm and steady; only then will you be able to think clearly.

But then, after you build a trading mindset, you must not let emotions play their role. However, the most common emotions that you must avoid are:

Euphoria

You might argue that euphoria is good, yes, it is good. But when it is related to the Forex market, it becomes dangerous. For example, if a trader wins a few profitable trades, he or she might become overconfident. It is good to feel confident when entering your trade, especially if you have done all your homework and analyses, but feeling overly confident is not. When traders become overly confident, they tend not to watch or study the market as carefully as they did before. When trading Forex if you are overconfident, you will not be able to accept the loss if the trade doesn't react the way you wanted. Hence, it is better to remain calm even if you make profits continuously.

Fear

Most traders who enter the market with no knowledge about trading tend to fear the market. Also, some traders might fear because they cannot effectively trade using any specific strategy. However, usually, when a trader continuously experiences losses, he or she may tend to fear to trade. Perhaps, it is understandable because losing hard-earned money isn't easy. But, you can avoid the mistake of risking more than the amount that you are comfortable with. Most naïve traders don't follow this rule even if we keep repeating it. If fear persists, you will not be able to trade better trades or become successful. It has the power to keep you away from good trades as well. Hence, try to overcome fear by limiting the amount you risk in trading. For the naïve traders, start your journey on a demo account without directly entering the live account. If you do so, you'll be able to learn to control emotions and learn how the market works without risking real money.

Greed

You might have heard that people say only bulls and bears make money, but pigs get slaughtered. If you don't understand what it means, it means greed. If you are greedy, you will not be able to make money. Instead, you will be kicked out of the market. Mostly, traders become greedy when they don't have self-discipline. Some traders make quick decisions when the market shows profitable trade signals, but it is not recommended. You should remain calm and collected, instead. Take some time to understand the market, focus on the risk ratio, set a plan, and then enter into the trade. Also, remember, if you are risking more than what you are ready to lose, this is usually indicates you're greedy. You must learn how to overcome greed if you don't want to blow your account and lose the money.

Revenge

This is one of the weird and funny behaviors some traders develop. What is the point in revenging the market? In the Forex market, you are just one amongst millions, and it doesn't make sense. If you are trying to revenge trade just because you lost a few trades, remember, this might very well lead to more losses. If you are emotional, you will not be able to make wise and rational decisions. Give yourself some time to calm down and regain stability and clarity before you start trading again.

Learning about yourself and the trading psychology might be exciting, but in order to do so correctly, it is better to take some of the pressure away, at least at the beginning. You don't have to try these tips and ideas on the live account, use the demo account instead. The Forex market is one of the best markets because it has solutions for almost all possible issues and, if you manage to solve your trading issues, it will help you become a successful trader.

Chapter 4. Winning Strategies

Step-By-Step Secrets Win

You are going to employ both fundamental and technical analysis to trade. This strategy is about utilizing all of the information that is at your fingertips to decide on a proper trading plan. You are still going to need to lay the groundwork for the currency pair you will trade; however, you will have steps to follow to ensure you are not exposing yourself to unnecessary risks. Your goal is to have a net profit for the year, not each week or each month. As long as your yearly P&L statement shows a profit, you have been successful. Determine your risk aversion. Are you a low, medium, or high risk taker? If you want to make modest money, but do not care to lose any money, then you need to place trades based on low risks.

Study the pairs you are interested in trading, whether it is the major currency pairs or major crosses. Understand the personalities of all the currencies in the pairs you are most likely to trade.

Assess when economic reports will be released. There are trade calendars that provide this data. Mark the most important economic reports on your calendar. If two countries have reports coming out on the same day, find out which report is more likely to affect price movement. USA labor reports will have a greater impact than Polish labor reports, particularly in the USA session.

Watch the news. Find out what news was released in other countries and what has happened in your own country since you went to bed. Are there any important events? For example, reports of fake bombs in the London Underground would have affected the European session, but three bombs, with one detonated in New Jersey, would have more of an impact on the USA session and the world.

Assess the charts for the top 3 currency pairs that have proper liquidity and volume for the day. Which charts are offering a clear pattern?

Based on your research, determine an entry point for one of the currency pairs.

Set the entry order.

Place a trailing stop order to protect your position.

Let the trade plan play out.

- Calculate your profit.
- Check for another entry/exit opportunity.
- Follow the above steps and start a new position, if the market provides an opportunity.

*Remember, you do not have to trade 365 days out of the year. You may find there are no currency pairs you are comfortable trading based on economic or technical market conditions. It is okay to not place a trade. You want to place trades based on the likelihood of success—not just to trade.

You have worked hard for your capital. You want to keep it. Make sure your emotions stay out of the mix. If you need to walk away from your computer and trading for an hour or several days, until a loss or significant profit is only a memory. The minute you let your emotions in and you start trading without a plan is the minute you will over leverage your account and lose all your capital, perhaps even more than that.

The Right Psychology of Success

It is an unusual experiment with the challenges of all our ideas on money. An auction of a 20-dollar bill. The rules are straightforward. The highest bidder gets 20 dollars. However, there is a catch; the second bidder gets nothing but pays the amount of the losing bid. Imagine a scenario where two participants bid way up the value of the 20 dollars. The question is, why would anyone pay more than 20 dollars for 20 dollars trying to cut his losses?

A series of rational bids will reach and ultimately surpass twenty dollars as the bidders seek to minimize their losses. If the first bidder bids 19 dollars 95 cents, and the second bidder bids twenty dollars (for no net gain or loss), the first bidder stands to lose 19 dollars 95 cents unless they bid $20.05, in which case they rationally bid more than the value of the item for sale (the 20 dollars) in order to reduce their losses to only 5 cents. Bidding continues with the second highest bidder always losing more than the highest bidder and therefore always trying to become the high bidder. Only the auctioneer gets to profit in the end.

Avoid The Get Rich Quick Mentality

Any time that people get involved with trading or investing, the hope is always there that there's a possibility of the big winning trade. It does happen now and then. But quite frankly, it's a rare event. In many occasions, even experienced traders are guessing wrong and taking losses. It's important to approach Forex for what it really is. It's a business. It is not a gambling casino even though a lot of people behave as if it was – it is a business no matter if you do it part-time, or quit your job and devote your entire life to it–and it has to be taken seriously. You wouldn't open a restaurant and recklessly buy 1 thousand pounds of lobster without seeing if customers were coming first. So, why would you approach Forex as if you were playing slots at the casino? Take it seriously and act as if was your own business because it really is. Again, it doesn't matter if you officially create a corporation to do your trades or not, it's still a business no matter what. That means you should approach things with care and avoid the get rich quick mentality. The fact is the get rich quick mentality never works anywhere. Unfortunately, I guess I could say I've been too strong in my assertion. It does work on rare occasions. It works well enough that it keeps the myth alive. But if we took 100 Forex traders who have to get rich quick mentality, my bet is within 90 days, 95% of them would be completely broke.

Trade Small

You should always trade small and set small achievable goals for your trading. The first benefit to trading small is that this approach will help you avoid a margin call. Second, it will also help you set profit goals that are small and achievable. That will help you stay in business longer.

Simply put, you will start gaining confidence and learning how to trade effectively if you get some trades that make $50 profits, rather than shooting for a couple of trades that would make thousands of dollars in one shot, but and up making you completely broke. Again, treat your trading like a real business. If you were opening a business, chances are you would start looking for slow and steady improvements and you certainly would not hope to get rich quick.

Let's get specific. Trading small means never trading standard lots. Even if you have enough cash to open an account such that you could trade standard lots, I highly recommend that you stay away from them. The large amount of capital involved and margin that would be used could just get you into a lot of financial trouble. For beginners, no matter how much money you are able to devote to your trading, I recommend that you start with micro lots. Take some time and learn how to trade with the small lots and start building your business earnings small profits at a time. Trading only with micro lots will help in force discipline and help you avoid getting into trouble. Make a commitment only to use micros for the first 60 days. After that, if you have been having decent success, consider trading a mini lot. You should be extremely cautious for the first 90 days in general.

Be Careful with Leverage

Obviously, it's extremely beneficial. It allows you to enter and trades that would otherwise not be possible. On the other hand, the temptation is there to use all your leverage in the hopes of making it big on one or two trades. You need to avoid using up all your leverage. Remember that you can have a margin call and get yourself into big trouble if your trades go bad. And it's important to remember there's a high probability that some of your trades are going to go bad no matter how carefully you do all your analysis.

Not Using a Demo Account

A big mistake the beginners make, is jumping in too quickly. There is a reason that most broker-dealers provide demos or simulated accounts. If you don't have a clue what that reason is, let's go ahead and stated here. Brokers provide demo accounts because Forex is a high-risk trading activity. It can definitely be something that provides a lot of rewards and it does for large numbers of traders. But there is a substantial risk of losing your capital. Many beginners are impatient hoping to make money right away. That's certainly understandable, but you don't want to fall into that trap. Take 30 days to practice with a demo account. This will provide several advantages. Trading on Forex is different than trading on the stock market. Using the demo account, you can become familiar with all the nuances of Forex trading. This includes everything from studying the charts, to placing your orders and, most importantly, understanding both pips and margin. The fact that there is so much leverage available means you need to learn how to use it responsibly. You need to know how to experience going through the process and reading the available margin and so forth on your trading platform while you are actually trying to execute trades. A demo account let you do this without risking real capital. It is true that it's not a perfect simulation. The biggest argument against demo accounts is that they don't incorporate the emotion that comes with trading and real money. As we all know, it's those emotions, including panic, fear and greed, that lead to bad decisions. However, in my opinion, that is a weak argument against using demo accounts. The proper way to approach it is to use a demo account for 30 days and then spend 60 to 90 days doing nothing but trading micro lots. Don't worry, as your micro trading lots you can increase the number of your trades and earn profits. While I know you're anxious to get started, keeping yourself from losing all your money is a good reason to practice for 30 days before doing it for real.

Failing to Check Multiple Indicators

There is also a temptation to get into trades quickly just on a gut level hunch. You need to avoid this approach at all costs. Some beginners will start learning about candlesticks and then when they first start trading, they will recognize a pattern on a chart. In the midst of the excitement, they will enter a large trade based on what they saw and finally end up on the losing end of a trade. Some people are even worse and they don't even look at the candlesticks. They just look at the trend and think they better get in on it quick. Before entering or exiting a position you should first check the candlesticks and then at least look for a confirmation by evaluating the moving average. You should also have the RSI handy and you may or may not want to use Bollinger bands.

Use Stop Loss and Take Profit Orders

Well, I hate to repeat myself yet again, but this point is extremely important. I am emphasizing it over and over because it's one of the tools that you can use in order to protect yourself from heavy losses. One of the ways that you can avoid having to worry about margin calls and running out of money is to put stop-loss orders every time you trade. This will require you to study the charts more carefully. You need to have know very clearly where you want to exit the trade, if it doesn't go the way you're expecting. If you place a stop-loss order, you will still lose but you will at least avoid catastrophic losses. Secondly, although you may always be tempted to make as much profit as you can, in most cases, you should also set a take profit order when you make your trade. In this way, you will set distinct boundaries which will ensure that you make some profit and limit your risk. The problem with doing it manually is that excitement and greed may interfere with your decisions and put you in a position where you risk missing your opportunities entirely. What inevitably happens, is people get too excited hoping to earn more profits and they stay in the trade too long. The Forex market changes very rapidly and if you stay too long you will almost inevitably end up losing, or at the very least miss out on profits.

There is one exception to this rule; a distinct and relatively long-term upward trend. If you perform a thorough analysis and determine the presence of such an upward trend, in that case only, you might want to try to ride the trend and maximize your profits.

Remember Price Changes Are in Pips

Beginners often make the mistake of forgetting about pips. If you have trouble with pips and converting them to actual money, go back and review the examples we provided. Remember that pips play a central role in price changes, you need to know your dollar value per pip in order to keep tabs on your profit and losses. This is also important for knowing the right stop loss and take profit orders to execute.

Don't Try Too Many Strategies or Trading Styles At Once

As a beginner in Forex trading you might be tempted to try everything under the sun. That can be overwhelming for most. The best thing you can do is to stick to one strategy and try to get proficient at it. Don't try scalping and position trading at the same time. The shorter the time frame for your trades, the more time and energy, you have to put into each trade. Scalping and day trading are activities that require a full-time commitment. They are also high-risk and high-pressure activities and can intensify emotions involved in the trades. For these reasons, I don't really recommend those styles or strategies for beginners. In my opinion and to be honest it's mine alone, I think position trading is also too much for a beginner. It requires too much patience. Perhaps the best strategy for a beginner in Forex trading is swing trading. It's a nice middle ground, in between the most extremely active trading styles and something that is going to try people's patience such as position trading. When you do swing trading, you can do time periods longer than a day certainly, but as long or short as you need to meet your goals otherwise. Swing trading also takes off some of the pressure. And it gives you more time to think and react.

This does not mean that you can't become a scalper or day trader at some future date. What I am advising is that you gain some experience using more relaxed trading styles before taking that path. And believe me, swing trading is going to be challenging enough.

Market Expectations

Life as a forex trader can sometimes get lonely. After all, this is the kind of career where you are completely on your own. You enjoy your profits alone, but you also suffer losses on your own. There is no one in the forex market whom you can depend on to comfort you. Therefore, it is also good if you connect with like-minded people. Feel free to make friends with other traders. After all, you are all players in the market who want the same thing. The good thing is that you are not competing with one another. In fact, you can even help one another by sharing information, insights, and strategies. Thanks to the Internet, it is very easy to find and connect with people who are also interested in forex trading. You simply have to join an online group or forum on forex trading. You can do this quickly with just a few clicks of a mouse. You can then make a public post or even send a private message to any member of the group/forum. If you have a neighbor or friend who also likes trading currencies, then you can invite him out for a coffee one of these days. Connecting with like-minded people is not just a way to learn but it can also inspire you to become a better trader.

Have Fun

Forex trading is fun. This is a fact. Many traders get to enjoy this lifestyle so much that they still continue despite their losses. It is also not uncommon to find traders, especially beginners, who spend their whole day just learning about forex trading. Like gambling in a casino, trading currencies can also be very addicting, especially if you are making a nice profit from it.

Learn to have fun and enjoy the journey. Sometimes taking things too seriously can ruin the experience and even make you less effective. In your life as a trader, you will definitely make some mistakes from time to time. You will experience losing money from what otherwise would have been a profitable trade if only you knew better. Do not get too stressed. The important thing is for you to learn as much as you can from every mistake. Take it easy, but remember to learn from experience. Making mistakes is part of the learning process. Of course, you should try to minimize them as much as possible by investing only sums of money you can afford to lose. Learn and have fun.

Chapter 5. Tips and Tricks

To the uninitiated, navigating the forex market successfully can seem like a difficult task. However, success is possible if one takes the right steps and trains properly. Just like training for a marathon, training is essential to winning in Forex Trading. Success requires targeted effort, practice, patience, and time.

Forex traders need to have specific goals in mind. With the right direction, training, and guidance, mastering the foreign exchange market is within anyone's reach. Winning at Forex Trading has little to do with hot picks, which are often fallacies created by people masquerading as experts in this field.

On the contrary, success stems from the ability to learn from both right and wrong trading choices to determine the patterns and strategies that work best for one's personality and goals. People are different; therefore, no single trading strategy will work for everyone.

Fortunately, there are several tips for winning in Forex Trading that can help beginners master the complexities of the largest market in the world. Actually, in terms of the value of average daily trading volume, the FX market dwarfs the bond and stock markets. Forex traders, therefore, have several inherent advantages over traders who engage in other forms of financial trading.

Small investors with modest capital can find success and trade their way to a fortune. The forex market is one of the few markets that can make this a reality. Trading the forex market is relatively easy. Doing it well and generating a consistent income, however, is not so easy. Therefore, it is important to learn the secrets and tips for success.

Tips and Secrets for Success

Pay Attention to Daily Pivot Points

Forex traders should watch daily pivot points closely. This is especially important for day traders. However, it is also important for swing traders, position traders, and even traders who focus on long-term positions. It is important to do so because tons of other forex traders do the same.

In a certain way, pivot trading is like a self-fulfilling prophecy. Essentially, markets often find resistance or support at pivot points since thousands of pivot traders place orders at those points. Consequently, when a large volume of trading moves happens at these points or levels, there is no other reason for the move except that many traders placed orders expecting such a move.

However, pivot points should not be the only basis of a Forex Trading strategy. Rather, regardless of one's strategy, one should watch these points for signs of either potential market or continuation of a trend. Forex traders should look at pivot levels and the trading activities that take place around them as a confirming indicator to use in conjunction with their chosen strategy.

Define Trading Style and Goals

Before setting out on any journey, travelers need to have a clear idea of where they are going and how to get to their destination. In the same way, forex traders need to have clear goals, in addition to ensuring that their trading strategies will help them achieve those goals.

Each Forex Trading style or strategy comes with a different risk profile. Therefore, traders who want to win in Forex Trading need to find and adopt the right approach and attitude to trade profitably. Those who cannot imagine going to sleep with an open market position, for example, should consider focusing on day trading.

Forex traders with funds they believe will benefit from a trade appreciation over several months; on the other hand, should think about position trading. Essentially, it is important for a forex trader to determine whether his/her personality will fit any particular trading strategy. Any mismatch will probably lead to certain losses and stress.

Trade with an Edge

Successful forex traders only risk their hard-earned money when a market opportunity provides them with an edge. In other words, they do so when the opportunity presents them with something that will boost the chances of their trades being successful. This edge can be various things, even a simple thing, such as selling at a price level that one identifies as strong resistance.

Forex traders can also increase their probability of success and their edge by having several technical factors in their favor. If the 100-period, 50-period, and 10-period moving averages all meet at the same price level, for example, it will likely offer significant resistance or support for a market because many traders will be acting together by trading off any of those averages.

Converging technical indicators also provide a similar edge. This happens when different indicators on many periods converge to provide resistance or support. Having the price hit an identified resistance or support level, in addition to having price movement at that level, is an indication of a potential market reversal.

The Trading Platform and Broker

Forex traders should spend adequate time researching a suitable trading platform and a reputable broker. It is important to identify and understand the difference between brokers and determine how each of them goes about making a market, as well as their policies. Trading the exchange-driven market, for example, is different from trading in the spot market or OTC market.

Traders should also choose the trading platform that fits the analysis they want to do. Traders who want to use Fibonacci numbers to trade, for example, should ensure the trading platform they choose has the ability to draw Fibonacci lives. A good platform with a bad broker is just as bad as a poor trading platform with a good broker. Therefore, forex traders need to find the best of both.

Preserve Capital

It is more important for traders to avoid huge losses than to make huge profits. For people who are new to Forex Trading, this concept may not sound quite right. However, it is important to understand that winning in Forex Trading means knowing how to preserve or protect one's capital.

According to the founder of Tudor Corporation, Paul Tudor Jones, playing great defense is the most important rule of trading. Actually, he is a great trader to learn from and study. In addition to building a hugely successful hedge fund, Tudor Jones has an excellent record of profitable trading.

He also played an important role in creating the ethics-training program needed to gain membership in all futures exchanges in the United States. Protecting the trading capital, or playing great defense, is very important in Forex Trading because many people who venture into Forex Trading are unable to continue trading as a result of running out of money.

Many forex traders drain their accounts soon after they make a few trades. Having strict risk management practices is important for people who want to win in Forex Trading. Traders who manage to preserve their trading capital are able to continue trading for as long as they want to, and might eventually become huge winners.

One great trade can fall into a trader's lap and significantly increase his/her profits and account size. One does not need to be the smartest trader in the world to make money in the forex market. If nothing else, the luck of the draw can have traders who manage to protect their capital stumble into trades that generate enough profits to make their trading careers a huge success.

Small Losses and Focus

After forex traders fund their trading accounts, they need to understand that their capital is at risk. Therefore, they should not depend on that money for their daily living expenses. Actually, it is better to think of those funds as vacation funds. Once their vacation is over, their money is gone.

Having this trading attitude will help prepare them to accept and learn from small losses, which will also help them manage their risk better. Forex traders should focus on their trades and accept small losses, which are normal in any type of business, rather than constantly and obsessively focusing on their equity.

Simple Technical Analysis

Consider this example of two forex traders in extremely different situations. The first trader has a specially designed trading computer with several monitors, a large office, swanky furnishings, trading charts, and market news feeds. He also has several moving averages, technical indicators, momentum indicators, and much more.

The other trader, on the other hand, works from a relatively simple office space and uses a regular desktop or laptop computer. His charts reveal just one or two technical indicators on the price action of the market.

Most people would consider the first trader to be more professional and extremely successful, and they would probably be wrong in their assumption. Actually, the second trader is closer to the image of a forex trader who wins consistently. Traders can apply numerous forms of technical analysis to a chart. Having more, however, does not necessarily mean having better.

Using a huge number of indicators might actually make things more complicated and confusing for a forex trader. They amplify indecision and doubt, causing him/her to miss many potentially profitable trades. Therefore, it is better to have a simple trading strategy with just a few rules, as well as a minimum of indicators to consider.

A few very successful forex traders make money from the forex market almost every day without using any technical indicators overlaid on their charts. They achieve this impressive feat without taking advantage of a relative strength indicator, trend lines, trading robots, moving averages, or expert advisors. Their market analysis involves a simple candlestick chart.

Weekend Analysis

The forex market ceases operation on the weekend (although the market is only closed to retail traders, forex trading takes place over the weekend through central banks and other organizations). Therefore, forex traders should use this time to study their weekly charts to identify news or patterns that could affect their trades in either a positive or a negative way. This will give the objectivity, which will help them make smarter trading plans.

Placing Stop-Loss Orders at the Right Price Levels

In addition to protecting one's capital in case of a losing trade, this strategy is also an important aspect of smart Forex Trading. Many newcomers to the forex market assume that risk management simply means placing stop-loss orders close to the entry point of their trades. This is partly accurate; however, habitually placing stop-loss orders too close to their trade entry points is something that might contribute to their lack of success. Sometimes, stop-loss orders can stop a trade, only to see the market make a reversal in favor of the trade. It is common for novice traders to endure watching this happen. Sometimes, this reversal proceeds to a level that would have seen them gain a sizable profit if the stop-loss order had not terminated the trade.

Obviously, traders should enter trades that allow them to place stop-loss orders close enough to their trade entry points to avoid making huge losses. However, they should place them at a reasonable price level, based on their analysis of the market. When it comes to reasonable placement of stop-loss orders, the general rule of thumb is to place them a bit further than the price the market should not trade at, based on market analysis.

Use a Consistent Methodology

Before a prospective trader enters the forex market, he/she needs to have a good idea of how he/she will make trading decisions. Essentially, forex traders should know the information they will need to make smart decisions on entering a trade or exiting one. Some traders choose to analyze a chart and the fundamental of the economy to decide the best time to trade.

Others, however, prefer to perform technical analysis to determine the ideal time to execute a trade. Whichever methodology or strategy a trader chooses to employ, he/she needs to be consistent and ensure the chosen methodology is adequately adaptive. In other words, it should be flexible enough to handle the forex market's changing dynamics.

Choosing the Right Entry and Exit Points

Most inexperienced forex traders do not know how to judge conflicting information that often presents when analyzing charts in various timeframes. Certain information, for example, might indicate a sell signal on a weekly chart, but show up as a purchasing opportunity in an intraday chart.

Therefore, if a trader is using a weekly chart to determine his/her basic trading direction and a daily chart to tie his/her entry, then he/she should try to synchronize the two charts. If the weekly chart is providing a buy signal, for example, he/she should wait for the daily chart to confirm this signal. In other words, keeping signal timing in sync is a good tip for winning in Forex Trading.

Calculating Expectancy

The formula to use to determine the reliability of a trading system is expectancy. Forex traders should analyze and compare past winning trades against losing trades, which will help them determine the profitability of their winning trades versus how much money they lost in their losing trades.

A simple way to do this is by looking at their last 10 trades. New forex traders who have not yet made any trades should study their chart to identify points where their trading system suggests an entry and/or exit point. In other words, new forex traders need to determine whether their system is profitable.

Having done this, they should write down their observations, total their winning trades, and divide the amount by the number of successful trades they made. For example, if a trader made 10 trades, four of which flopped, and six of which were successful, his/her win ratio would be 60% or 6/10. If the six winning trades made $4,800, then his/her average win would be $4,800/6 = $800.

If the trader's losses amounted to $2,400, then his/her average loss would be $2,400/4 = $600. By applying these results to the formula for calculating the reliability of a system, the trader will get E = [1 + (800/600) x 0.6 – 1 = 0.4, which is equivalent to 40%. A positive expectancy of 40% means that the trader's trading system will likely generate 40 cents to the dollar over the long term.

Positive Feedback Loops

Forex traders create a positive feedback loop following a well-planned and executed trade. When they plan a trade and execute it as expected, traders tend to create a pattern of positive feedback. In other words, success tends to breed success, which, in turn, builds confidence. This is especially true if the trade generates significant profits. Even if a trader suffers a small loss following a well-planned trade, he/she will still build a positive feedback loop.

Keeping Printed Records

Printed records serve as a good learning tool for forex traders. Therefore, traders, especially new ones, should print their charts create a list of reasons for any particular trade, including the things that sway their trading decisions. They should mark the entry and exit points on the chart and make any relevant comments, such as emotional reasons for taking specific actions.

Forex traders need to objectify their trades to develop the discipline and mental control needed to execute trades according to their systems, instead of their emotions, greed, or habits.

Stress Less

This is an obvious Forex Trading tip. Trading the forex market under stress tends to lead to irrational decisions, which can end up costing a trader a lot of money. Therefore, forex traders should identify the source of their stress and try to get rid of it, or at least limit its influence on their actions.

When stress threatens to take control, a trader should take deep breaths and try to focus on other things for a few minutes. People have different ways of overcoming stress. Some exercise, while others listen to classical music. Traders should learn what works best for them.

Conclusion

Congratulations for making it to the end of this book! I know it was a lot of information for you to take in, so this is really an accomplishment in your swing trading career!

One of the goals of this book was to give you a start on your swing trading career. Not only did I want to explain the key concepts of financial trading. Because this is considered to be a foundation when it comes to trading, I didn't want to leave this information out of the book. On top of this, it was important to explain to you the difference between trading and investing. There are a lot of people who get into trading when they believed they were going to be investing money instead of trading stocks in order to gain a profit. Because these two topics are different, it is important to make sure you want to be a trader and not an investor before you go too far into your research for swing trading.

Another major point of this book was to give you a concise beginner's guide about swing trading which touched on a variety of topics. Instead of you having to read dozens more articles and a few books about swing trading, I wanted to give you a way that you can place one book in your device to turn to when you need a refresher about swing trading. On top of this, I wanted you to be able to show this book to your friends who are interested in swing trading and show them this beginner's guide, so they can get all the information required before opening their account with a broker.

As you have realized by this point, swing trading is not the easiest career; however, when it comes to the forex market, there is no easy career. It doesn't matter if you decide on swing trading, become a buy and hold investor, or get into day trading, you will find that each one of these areas has its own challenges. However, you will soon come to find that they also have their advantages. You should already to be able to pick out a few advantages to becoming a swing trader. For example, you could one day be able to trade without the assistance of a broker. On top of this, you have been able to get a sneak peak of the many online communities for swing traders. Once you decide to join an online community or two, you will realize how enjoyable swing trading is.

You should also understand what simulation trading is and how important it is to make sure you complete this type of trading before you start trading for money. You should also not only understand risks which are associated in swing trading but also have an idea on how to decrease these risks once you start swing trading. Of course, this is one reason you want to make sure to practice trading in demo mode at first. As stated before, simulation trading will help you make sure that you understand the risks and strategies associated with swing trading and get a general feeling of how the market works.

By now you should not only clearly understand what swing trading is, but also what the average time frame for a swing trader is. You should be able to remember the 11 commandments of swing trading, techniques, what the right mindset is when you are trading, know a variety of tips to help you get on your way, and also understand the many mistakes that other swing traders have made.

Furthermore, you should be able to explain how a day will go for a full-time swing trader, be able to explain the two different types of stock market conditions, and the art of short selling.

On top of all the information you need to know about being a swing trader, you also know how to get started with researching as much information as possible. On top of this, you have learned tips to help you become a better researcher, so you can gain the most out of your research time. It is important to keep these tips in mind as you will need to used them throughout your career. On top of this, you can also add your own tips, which will become useful when you begin to help other beginner swing traders in the next few years.

Thank you for not only purchasing this book but also reading it. I hope that you found it helpful in your swing trading journey. I wish you the best of luck!

www.ingramcontent.com/pod-product-compliance
Lightning Source LLC
Chambersburg PA
CBHW081746200326
41597CB00024B/4413